Kindle Fire™ HD
FOR
DUMMIES®
PORTABLE EDITION

by Nancy C. Muir and Harvey Chute

WILEY

John Wiley & Sons, Inc.

Kindle Fire™ HD For Dummies®, Portable Edition

Published by
John Wiley & Sons, Inc.
111 River Street
Hoboken, NJ 07030-5774

www.wiley.com

Copyright © 2013 by John Wiley & Sons, Inc., Hoboken, New Jersey

Published by John Wiley & Sons, Inc., Hoboken, New Jersey

Published simultaneously in Canada

For general information on our other products and services, please contact our Customer Care Department within the U.S. at 877-762-2974, outside the U.S. at 317-572-3993, or fax 317-572-4002.

For technical support, please visit www.wiley.com/techsupport.

Wiley publishes in a variety of print and electronic formats and by print-on-demand. Some material included with standard print versions of this book may not be included in e-books or in print-on-demand. If this book refers to media such as a CD or DVD that is not included in the version you purchased, you may download this material at http://booksupport.wiley.com. For more information about Wiley products, visit www.wiley.com.

ISBN 978-1-118-53074-0 (pbk); ISBN 978-1-118-54706-9 (ebk); ISBN 978-1-118-54710-6 (ebk); ISBN 978-1-118-54715-1 (ebk)

Manufactured in the United States of America

10 9 8 7 6 5 4 3 2

WILEY

About the Authors

Nancy Muir is the author of over 100 technology books on topics ranging from tablet computers and popular computer applications to nanotechnology. Her website TechSmart Senior (www.techsmartsenior.com) provides information for those reading her bestselling *Computers For Seniors For Dummies* and *Laptops For Seniors For Dummies* books (both published by Wiley) and others discovering technology later in their lives. She contributes a column on computers and the Internet at www.retirenet.com. Prior to her writing career, Nancy was a manager in both the publishing and computer software industries.

Harvey Chute created the independent Kindle discussion forum, KindleBoards (www.kindleboards.com). The site is an active hub for Kindle owners, with 60,000 registered members and more than a million posts about all things Kindle. As a lover of reading, innovative technology, and gadgets, Harvey has had a natural passion for Amazon's Kindle since the first generation of the device was released in 2007.

Harvey is a program manager for a systems integration company. He is the author or technical editor of seven other *For Dummies* books. His interests include software development, reading, music, photography, and enjoying life with his wife and three daughters.

Table of Contents

Chapter 6: E-Reader Extraordinaire 79

Chapter 7: Playing Music 95

Chapter 8: Playing Video 105

Chapter 9: Going Social 113

Publisher's Acknowledgments

We're proud of this book; please send us your comments at http://dummies.custhelp.com. For other comments, please contact our Customer Care Department within the U.S. at 877-762-2974, outside the U.S. at 317-572-3993, or fax 317-572-4002.

Some of the people who helped bring this book to market include the following:

Acquisitions, Editorial, and Media Development

Project Editor and Copy Editor: Susan Christophersen

Acquisitions Editor: Katie Mohr

Editorial Assistant: Leslie Saxman

Cover photo: © iStockphoto.com / TUNA TIRKAZ

Composition Services

Sr. Project Coordinator: Kristie Rees

Layout and Graphics: Carrie A. Cesavice, Christin Swinford

Proofreader: Linda Seifert

Indexer: Potomac Indexing, LLC

Publishing and Editorial for Technology Dummies

Richard Swadley, Vice President and Executive Group Publisher

Andy Cummings, Vice President and Publisher

Mary Bednarek, Executive Acquisitions Director

Mary C. Corder, Editorial Director

Publishing for Consumer Dummies

Kathleen Nebenhaus, Vice President and Executive Publisher

Composition Services

Debbie Stailey, Director of Composition Services

Introduction

*T*he Kindle Fire HD is a very affordable way to obtain and enjoy all kinds of media, from music and videos to books and colorful magazines. It's also a device that allows you to browse the Internet, connect to your Facebook account, make video calls via Skype, check your e-mail, and read documents. Its portability makes it incredibly useful for people on the go in today's fast-paced world.

In this book, we introduce you to all the cool features of the Fire HD, providing tips and advice for getting the most out of this ingenious little tablet. We help you find your way around its attractive and easy-to-use interface, provide advice about getting the most out of the Amazon Cloud feature for storing and using content, and even recommend some neat apps that make your device more functional and fun.

Why Buy This Book?

"If the Kindle Fire HD is so easy to use, why do I need a book?" you may be asking yourself. When we first sat down with the Kindle Fire, it took about three or four days of poking around to find settings, features, and ways to buy and locate content and apps. When was the last time you had four days to spare? We've spent the time so that you can quickly and easily get the hang of all the Kindle Fire HD features and discover a few tricks that we bet your friends won't uncover for quite a while.

 This book covers many of the features in the original Kindle Fire released in 2011 as well as the features that are new with the Kindle Fire HD. In September 2012, Amazon also released a new version of the non-HD Fire (sometimes referred to as the Kindle Fire SD) that costs $159 and has only 8GB of storage along with the somewhat clunkier hardware design of the original Kindle Fire. Though this book is focused on the Kindle Fire HD, whichever Kindle Fire model you own, you should find lots of advice and answers in this book.

Foolish Assumptions

You may have opted for a tablet to watch movies and read books on the run. You might think it's a good way to browse business documents and check e-mail on your next plane trip. Perhaps you have one or more computers and are very computer savvy, or you hate computers and figure that the Kindle Fire HD gives you all the computing power you need to browse the Internet and read e-books.

Kindle Fire HD users come in all types. We don't assume in this book that you're a computer whiz, but we do assume that you have a passing understanding of how to copy a file and plug in a USB cable. We're guessing that you've browsed the Internet at least a few times and heard of Wi-Fi, which is what you use to go online with a Kindle Fire HD (unless you purchase the 8.9 inch LTE version). Other than our assumptions mentioned here, you don't need a lot of technical background to get the most out of this book.

How This Book Is Organized

For Dummies books don't require a linear read, meaning that you can jump in anywhere and find out what you need to know about a particular feature. However, if you're opening the box and starting from square one with your Kindle Fire HD, consider working through the first couple of chapters first. They provide information about setting up your Kindle Fire HD and navigating your way around its interface.

Subsequent chapters help you go online and set up your e-mail account and Wi-Fi connection. Then we begin to explore the wealth of multimedia and written content that the Kindle Fire HD makes available to you. We even include two chapters at the end of the book that recommend apps for adding basic functionality to the Kindle Fire HD, such as a calculator and notes, along with ten games to turn your Kindle Fire HD into a great gaming machine.

Icons Used in This Book

Icons are little pictures in the margin of this book that alert you to special types of advice or information, including

✔ These short paragraphs of advice draw your attention to faster, easier, or alternative ways of getting something done with the Kindle Fire HD.

✔ When you see this icon, you know that we're emphasizing important information for you to keep in mind as you use a feature.

✔ You don't have many ways to get in trouble with the Kindle Fire HD, but in those few situations in which some action might be irreversible, we include warnings so that you avoid any pitfalls.

Get Going!

Time to get that Kindle Fire HD out of its box, set it up, and get going with all the fun, productive, and entertaining activities it makes available to you. Have fun!

Look for updates on Dummies.com when the new Kindles come out in the fall of 2013.

Chapter 1

Overview of the Kindle Fire HD

In This Chapter

▶ Comparing Kindle Fire HD to the competition

▶ Surveying all the features of the Kindle Fire HD

*A*mazon, the giant online retailer, has access to more content (music, movies, audiobooks, and so on) than just about anybody on the planet. So when an Amazon tablet was rumored to be in the works, the mystery tablet was seen as the first real challenge to the Apple iPad.

Now, a year after the release of the first Kindle Fire, the Kindle Fire HD is available, and it turns out to offer several very nice improvements over the original. It has the right price and feature mix for many people while also offering the key to that treasure chest of Amazon content.

In this chapter, you get an overview of the Kindle Fire HD: how it compares to competing devices as well as a look at its key features. Subsequent chapters delve into how to use all those features.

A Quick Rundown of Kindle Fire HD Hardware Features

A *tablet* is a handheld computer with a touchscreen and an onscreen keyboard for providing input, and apps that allow you to play games, read e-books, check e-mail, browse the web, and more.

In the world of tablets, the first device to hit the big time was iPad, after which subsequent tablets, such as Samsung Galaxy, Google Nexus 7, and HP TouchPad, appeared. No tablet since iPad seemed to gain a foothold in the market until the Kindle Fire showed up.

The Kindle Fire HD, the second generation of the Kindle Fire, is lighter and smaller than the iPad, at 7.6 x 5.4 x 0.4 inches (see Figure 1-1) and weighing only 13.9 ounces, versus the iPad's 9.7-inch display and 1.3-pound frame. For some, that smaller, lighter form factor makes the Kindle Fire HD easier to hold with one hand than the iPad. In addition, the rubberized back helps you keep a tight grip on the device in most circumstances.

The Kindle Fire HD has a projected battery life of 11 hours. The screen resolution on the Kindle Fire HD's bright color screen is on par with the best tablets out there.

In its first-generation model, the Kindle Fire had no camera and no microphone. With the arrival of the Kindle Fire HD, you have a camera and microphone that are useful mainly for making video calls with the built-in Skype app.

Although a micro-USB cord is included with the Kindle Fire HD, no power adapter for plugging it into an outlet and charging it comes with the package. You can buy an adapter from Amazon for about $10 when you buy your device, or for $20 separately. Alternatively, you can root around in your kitchen drawer to see whether you have ever owned a smartphone that came with such an adapter. The adapter simply plugs into the USB end of the micro-USB cable.

Figure 1-1: The neat size and weight of Kindle Fire HD make it easy to hold.

Table 1-1 provides an at-a-glance view of Kindle Fire HD features.

Table 1-1	Kindle Fire HD Specifications
Feature	**Kindle Fire HD Specs**
Display size	7 inches or 8.9 inches
Processor	Dual Core Omap 4470 processor
Screen resolution	7 inch: 1280 x 800
	8.9 inch: 1900 x 1200
Internal storage	7 inch: 16 or 32GB
	8.9 inch: 32 or 64GB
Battery life	11 hours
Price	7 inch: $199 for 16GB and $249 for 32GB
	8.9 inch: $299 for 16GB and $369 for 32GB
	8.9 inch 4G LTE: $499 for 32GB and $599 for 64GB
Content	Amazon Appstore
Connectivity	Wi-Fi
	4G LTE for 8.9 inch 4G LTE model
Ports	USB 2.0, mini USB
Browser	Silk
Camera	Video calls and still photos
Sound	Dual stereo speakers, Dolby Digital Plus sound
Volume rocker	Physical volume rocker switches
Antenna	Dual band, dual antenna for Wi-Fi

Key Features of Kindle Fire HD

Kindle Fire HD is a tablet device with all the things most people want from a tablet packed into an easy-to-hold package. In the following sections, you get to explore some of the Kindle Fire HD's great features.

Storage on earth and in the Amazon Cloud

Kindle Fire HD offers 16 to 32GB of storage in its 7" model. Either storage amount will probably work just fine for you because when you own a Kindle Fire HD, you get free, unlimited Amazon Cloud storage for all digital content purchased from Amazon. *Cloud storage* means that books, movies, music, and apps are held online for you to stream or download at any time, so you don't have to store it on your Kindle Fire HD.

If you'll be away from an Internet connection, download an item (such as an episode of your favorite TV show), watch it, and then remove it from your device. The content is still available in the Amazon Cloud Player, and you can download that content again or stream it anytime you like.

 If you want to go whole hog into Kindle Fire HD land, you can opt for the highest memory device, the 64GB 8.9" 4G LTE Wireless version of the device. Just be aware that this version comes with the cost of an AT&T account for the 4G LTE access.

App appeal

Kindle Fire HD comes with built-in functions and apps like the Silk web browser, an e-mail client, calendar and contact apps, a Skype app, and the Kindle e-reader (see Figure 1-2). Many more apps are readily available from the Amazon Appstore.

 At this point, the selection of apps available for Android devices isn't quite as robust as those available for Apple devices, but that will change over time. See Chapter 11 for ten apps that can flesh out your Kindle Fire HD with popular features, and check out Chapter 12 for ten great game apps.

Check out the price

Amazon brought the Kindle Fire to market as a lower-priced device. Some consider it just a device for buying Amazon content, and it certainly lacks some features of more sophisticated devices such as the iPad. However, the lower pricing scheme has clearly been a hit with many people.

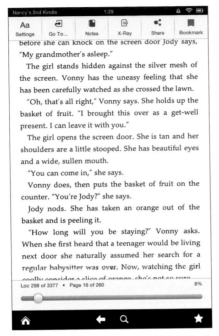

Figure 1-2: Where it all started, with Kindle e-reader functionality.

At the top end, you'll pay $829 for a 64GB 3G iPad, compared to $599 for an 8.9" 4G LTE Kindle Fire HD. Amazon is positioning its device as a more cost-effective tablet, but do be aware that the lower cost on the Kindle Fire HD is subsidized by on-device advertising. You can pay $15 to have the advertising removed from your Kindle Fire HD experience. To send those ads packing, go to the Manage Your Kindle page on Amazon (http://amazon.com/myk) and click the Unsubscribe link by the device. Note that this action does not remove the Customers Also Bought banner that appears on your Home screen, but it does remove the Special Offers notices that appear when the device is in sleep mode.

Pre-installed functionality

Here's a rundown of the functionality you get out of the box from pre-installed apps:

- ✔ E-reader for use with both books and periodicals
- ✔ Music player

- ✔ Video player
- ✔ Audiobook player
- ✔ Contacts app
- ✔ Calendar app
- ✔ Document reader for Word, PDF, RTF, and HTML files
- ✔ The Amazon Silk web browser
- ✔ Photos viewer
- ✔ The IMDb database of movie trivia and facts
- ✔ E-mail client
- ✔ Integration for Facebook and Twitter
- ✔ OfficeSuite for simple word processing and spreadsheet functionality

Check out the available apps! Tap Apps on the home screen and then tap Store. Here you find a number of free apps such as a Wi-Fi analyzer to check your Wi-Fi connection, free games, and more.

Kindle Fire HD gives you the ability to

- ✔ Shop at Amazon for music, video, apps, books, and periodicals and to view or play that content.
- ✔ Store Amazon-purchased content in the Amazon Cloud and play music and video selections from the Cloud rather than download them to your device. Amazon content doesn't count toward your Cloud storage limit (20GB), but other content that's backed up there does.
- ✔ Send documents to yourself at a Kindle e-mail address that's assigned when you register your device (see Chapter 3 for more about your Kindle e-mail address).
- ✔ Make video calls using the free, available Skype for Kindle Fire HD app.
- ✔ Transfer content from your computer to your Kindle Fire HD by using the micro-USB cable that came with your device. Using this cable (see Figure 1-3), you can copy photos, music, videos, and documents (Word or PDF) from any source onto your Kindle Fire HD.

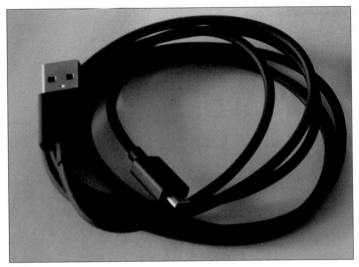

Figure 1-3: The micro-USB cable, included with Kindle Fire HD.

The magic of Whispersync

If you've ever owned a Kindle e-reader, you know that downloading Amazon content to it has always been seamless. All you need for this process is access to a Wi-Fi network. Kindle Fire HD enjoys the same kind of easy download capability. You simply order a book, music, or a video, and within moments, the item appears on your tablet.

Whispersync also helps to sync items such as bookmarks that you've placed in e-books. Additionally, it syncs to where you left off in a book or video, and it does this across various devices that you use. For example, say that you have the Kindle e-reader app on your Kindle Fire HD, PC, and smartphone. Wherever you left off reading, whatever notes you entered, and whatever pages you bookmarked will be synced among all the devices you use without your having to lift a finger.

A great addition to the Kindle Fire HD is something called Immersion Reading. This feature lets you listen to an audiobook and have the current word that's being spoken highlighted in the text. A nice feature for those late-night study sessions with textbooks!

Content, content, content!

Kindle Fire HD lets you easily consume media, meaning that you can play or read all kinds of music, movies, TV shows, podcasts, e-books, audiobooks, magazines, and newspapers. Amazon has built up an immense collection of content (more than 22 million movies, TV shows, songs, books, magazines, audiobooks, apps, and games). These numbers are rising all the time, too. Figure 1-4 shows the opening screen for the well-stocked Kindle store.

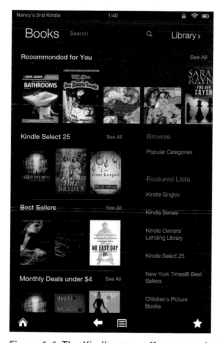

Figure 1-4: The Kindle store offers more than 1 million books for the Kindle e-reader app.

Tap a library such as Books, Music, or Videos on the Kindle Fire HD home screen. Tap Newsstand to view periodicals; tap Music to view songs and albums; tap Video to watch videos; and tap Apps to view your downloaded applications. From each of those screens, you can find additional content in the Amazon store by tapping the Store in the top-right corner of the screen.

If you have an Amazon Prime membership, you can also take advantage of the Kindle Owner's Lending Library. This service lets you choose from more than 190,000 books that you can borrow at no charge for as long as you like. Amazon Prime members can borrow one book a month.

If you're concerned about kids who access content over your Kindle Fire HD, check out the limitations you can put in place using Parental Controls, which we cover in Chapter 3.

You can also transfer documents from your computer or send them via e-mail and read them on Kindle Fire HD or share them via Amazon Cloud. Note, however, that those personal docs are not backed up in the Amazon Cloud.

Browsing with Amazon Silk

Silk is Kindle Fire HD's browser (see Figure 1-5). Silk is simple to use, but the real benefits of Amazon Silk are all about browsing performance.

Figure 1-5: Amazon Silk offers simple-to-use browsing tools.

Amazon Silk is touted as a "cloud-accelerated split browser." The browser uses the power of Amazon's servers to load pages of a website quickly. Because the page-loading process is partly handled by servers in the Amazon Cloud, your pages simply display faster.

In addition, you get what's called a persistent connection, which means that your tablet is always connected to the Amazon Internet backbone (the routes over which data travels to move among networks online) whenever it has access to a wireless connection.

A world of color on the durable display

The display on Kindle Fire HD 7-inch model offers a 1280 x 800 HD display (see Figure 1-6). The high-resolution screen makes for crisp colors when you're watching that hit movie or reading a colorful magazine. *In-plane switching* is a technology that gives you a wide viewing angle on the Kindle Fire HD screen. So if you want to share your movie with a friend sitting next to you on the couch, she'll have no problem seeing what's on the screen from that side angle.

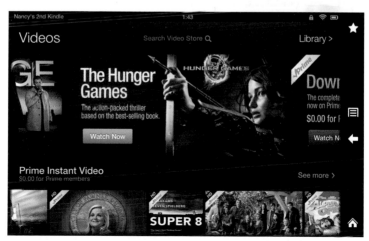

Figure 1-6: The bright display on Kindle Fire HD makes media shine.

Of course, you should avoid dropping your Kindle Fire HD, exposing it to extreme temperatures, or spilling liquids on it. Perhaps anticipating the temporary insanity of a panicky moment, the User Guide also advises that if you do spill liquids, you shouldn't heat the device in your microwave to dry it off.

Understanding the Value of Amazon Prime

Kindle Fire HD comes with one free month of Amazon Prime. If you decide to pick up the service after your free month, it currently will cost you $79 a year. So what do you get for your money?

Prime includes free two-day shipping on millions of items and overnight shipping for only $3.99. Not every item offered on Amazon is eligible for Prime, but enough are that it's a wonderful savings in time and money over the course of a year. You can probably pay for the membership with the free shipping on the first few orders you place. And getting your Amazon orders in only two days every time is sweet.

In addition, Prime membership gives you access to Prime Instant Videos, which includes thousands of movies and TV shows that you can stream to your Kindle Fire HD absolutely free. We're not talking obscure 1970s sleepers here: Recent additions to Prime Instant Videos include TV series such as *Sherlock* and *Man vs. Wild,* and popular movies such as *Iron Man 2, Mission Impossible 3,* and *Winter's Bone.*

If you don't have a Prime account, your 30 days for the free account starts from the time you activate your Kindle Fire HD, not the first time you make a Prime purchase. We recommend that you start using it right away to take full advantage and decide whether the paid membership is for you.

You can connect a cable from your TV to the HDMI port on your Kindle Fire to play movies stored on your device or in the cloud on the television. The HDMI port is used to send information about the video to your TV's video receiver.

Chapter 2
Kindle Fire HD Quick Start

*1*n this chapter, we familiarize you with what comes in the box, explore the interface (what you see on the screen), and start to use your fingers to interact with the touchscreen. Finally, to round out your introduction to Kindle Fire HD basics, you begin to get a sense of how things are organized on the Kindle Fire HD Home screen.

Get Going with Kindle Fire HD

This section examines what comes in the Kindle Fire HD box and tells you how to turn your nifty new device on and off. The first time you turn on Kindle Fire HD, you register it and link it to your Amazon account so that you can shop till you drop.

Opening the box

When your Kindle Fire HD arrives, it will come in a dark-gray box. The Kindle Fire HD itself rests on top of a piece of hard plastic, and a small, black card with some Kindle Fire HD basic information is slotted into the box lid. Finally, beneath the plastic rests a charger in a paper sleeve. That's it.

Turning your Kindle Fire HD on and off

The Kindle Fire HD sports a Power button on the top of the device when you hold it in portrait orientation (see Figure 2-1). Next to the Power button is a volume rocker and a headphone jack.

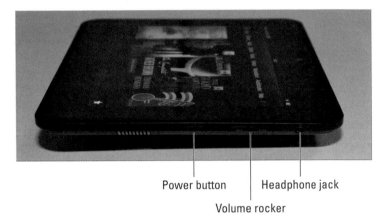

Power button | Headphone jack

Volume rocker

Figure 2-1: The Power button sits on the top of your Kindle Fire HD.

To turn the device on, press the Power button. If you're starting your Kindle Fire HD for the first time, you're taken through a series of setup screens, described in the following section. After you've registered your device, you see the Home screen shown in Figure 2-2 on startup.

If you want to lock your Kindle Fire HD, which is akin to putting a laptop computer to sleep to conserve battery charge, tap the Power button again. To shut down your Kindle, press and hold the Power button until a message appears with options to Shut Down or Cancel.

If your Kindle Fire HD becomes nonresponsive, press and hold the Power button for 20 seconds; it should come to life again.

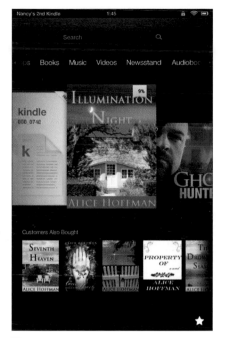

Figure 2-2: The Kindle Fire HD Home screen.

Getting to know the touchscreen

Before you work through the setup screens, it helps to get to know the basics of navigating the touchscreen:

- Swipe your finger down from the top of the Home screen to display Quick Settings; swipe up again to hide the Settings.

- Tap an item to select it or double-tap an item to open it.

- If your Kindle Fire HD goes to a lock screen after a period of inactivity, swipe your finger from right to left across the band with the padlock icon (see Figure 2-3). You can also swipe your finger from left to right to see details about the latest ad displayed there.

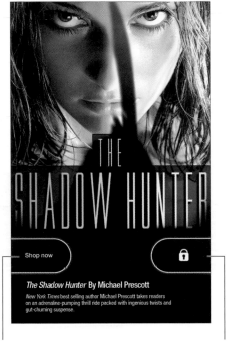

See ad details   Go to Home screen

Figure 2-3: Swipe right to left from the padlock icon to go to the Home screen.

- ✔ When viewing a web page, you can double-tap to enlarge text and double-tap again to return the text to its original size.

- ✔ Place your fingers apart on a screen and pinch them together to zoom in on the current view; move them apart (unpinch) to enlarge the view.

- ✔ Swipe left to move to the next page in the e-reader. Swipe right to move to the previous page.

- ✔ Swipe up and down to scroll up and down a web page.

These touchscreen gestures are the ones that help you get around most of the content and setup screens you encounter in Kindle Fire HD.

Setting up your Kindle Fire HD

When you turn on the Kindle Fire HD for the first time, you see a series of screens that help you set up and register the device.

 At some point during this setup procedure, you may be prompted to plug in your adapter if your battery charge is low. You may also be notified that the latest Kindle software is downloading and you have to wait for that process to complete before you can move forward.

This is the point in the setup process at which you connect to a wireless network. Follow these steps to register and set up your Kindle Fire HD:

1. **In the Connect to a Network list, tap an available network.**

   Kindle Fire HD connects to the network (you may need to enter a password and then tap Connect to access an available network) and then displays the Time Zone screen.

2. **Tap to select a time zone from the list provided.**

   For countries other than the United States, tap More and choose from the provided list.

3. **Tap Continue.**

4. **On the Register Your Kindle screen that appears (see Figure 2-4), enter your Amazon account information, e-mail address, and your Amazon account password; then skip to Step 7.**

   See Step 5 if you don't have an Amazon account.

5. **If you don't have an Amazon account, click the New to Amazon? Create an Account link.**

   This link takes you to the Create an Amazon Account screen, with fields for entering your name, e-mail address, and password.

6. **Enter this information and then tap Continue.**

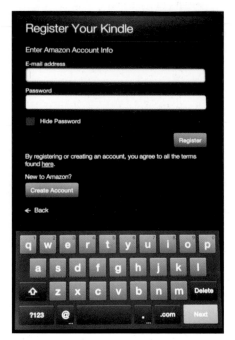

Figure 2-4: Register your Kindle Fire HD to use it.

7. **If you want to read the terms of registration, tap the By Registering, You Agree to All of the Terms Found Here link. Tap the Close button to return to the registration screen.**

8. **To complete the registration, tap the Register button.**

   A final screen appears saying Welcome to Kindle Fire HD: Hello *<Your Name>*.

Tap the Get Started Now button and you can view a series of tips to get you started with Kindle Fire HD, as shown in Figure 2-5. Tap Next to move through this tour; on the last of the three screens, tap Close to get going with Kindle Fire HD.

You can also register an account at a later time by swiping down on the Home screen to display the Quick Settings, tapping More, and then tapping My Account. Tap the Register button on the next screen and enter your account information.

Figure 2-5: This brief tutorial covers the basics of using Kindle Fire HD.

Charging the battery

You get about 11 hours of reading downloaded books, even with wireless turned on. (You can get even more battery life by turning the wireless connection off.)

Charge the battery by using the provided micro-USB cord, which can be plugged into any standard USB charger or into a computer with the newer USB 2.0 ports.

For a faster charge, you can get a powerful charging adapter from Amazon. Attach the smaller end of the charger to your Kindle Fire HD's micro-USB port, on the right side of the device, and the other end to the power adapter; then plug it in to a wall outlet. If Kindle Fire HD is completely out of juice, you need about four hours to charge it.

Getting to Know the Interface

The interface that you see on the Kindle Home screen (see Figure 2-6) is made up of four items. At the top is a Search field that allows you to search all your content and apps. Next you see links that take you to the various Kindle Fire HD libraries. In the middle of the screen is the Carousel, with images of items you recently used. Finally, the bottom portion of the Home screen contains a Customers Also Bought listing of other items that Amazon imagines you might enjoy based on your other purchases.

Library items

Carousel

Customers Also Bought

Figure 2-6: This graphical interface is fun to move around in with the flick of a finger.

Understanding how the Amazon Cloud works with the Kindle Fire HD

When you purchase content from Amazon, you can choose whether to keep it only in the Amazon Cloud or also download it to your Kindle Fire HD. If you download it, you can access it regardless of whether you're in range of a wireless network. At any time, you can remove content from the device, and it will remain archived in the Cloud for you to later stream to your device (music or video) or redownload (music, video, books, and magazines). Removing content from your device that you're not currently using saves space on your device.

Accessing Kindle Fire HD libraries

Kindle Fire HD libraries are where you access content and go online to browse and buy more content.

Tap any library item: Games, Apps, Books, Music, Videos, Newsstand, Audiobooks, or Photos.

The Video app opens to the Amazon store rather than a library. Because this type of content takes up a lot of memory, it's generally preferable to play video from Amazon's Cloud (which is called *streaming*) rather than to download it to your device.

 Among the library links is also a Web link that you can tap to open the Silk web browser. Find out more about going online and using the browser in Chapter 5.

Within a library, such as the Music library shown in Figure 2-7, you can tap Device or Cloud. The Device button shows you only content you have downloaded; the Cloud button displays all your content stored in Amazon's Cloud library, regardless of whether you've downloaded it.

You can view the contents of libraries in different ways, depending on which library you're in. For example, you can view Music library contents by categories such as Playlists, Artists, Albums, and Songs.

Figure 2-7: Your Music library provides access to all your musical content.

See Chapter 4 for more about buying content, Chapter 6 for information about reading books and magazines, and Chapters 7 and 8 for more about playing music and video.

You can also transfer content that you've obtained from other sources, such as iTunes, to your Kindle Fire HD libraries. See the section "Using a Micro-USB Cable to Transfer Data," later in this chapter, for more about this process.

Playing with the Carousel

The Kindle Fire HD Carousel is a revolving display of recent books, audiobooks, music, videos, websites, docs, and apps (see Figure 2-8).

Items you've used recently are displayed here chronologically, with the most recent item you used on top. Swipe your finger to the right or left to flick through the Carousel contents. See an item you want to view or play? Just tap to open it.

Figure 2-8: The Kindle Fire HD's Carousel makes recently used content available.

When you first begin using the Kindle Fire HD, the Carousel contains the Amazon Kindle User Guide and the absolutely free New Oxford American Dictionary. It may also contain recently used content from your Amazon Cloud library.

Organizing Favorites

Over time, the Carousel can get a bit crowded. You may have to swipe five or six times to find what you need. That's where Favorites comes in.

Favorites is a way of getting to frequently used content. If, for example, you're reading a book that you open often or you play a certain piece of music frequently, place it in the Favorites area of the Kindle Fire HD to find it quickly.

To pin an item to the Favorites area, press and hold it in the Carousel or a library and then select Add to Favorites from the menu that appears.

To remove content from Favorites, press and hold the item; then choose Remove from Favorites in the menu that appears.

Getting info about your device from the Status bar

The Status bar runs across the top of every Kindle Fire HD screen. This bar, shown in Figure 2-9, provides information about the time, your network connection, and your battery charge.

Figure 2-9: The various tools and settings available on the Status bar.

Here's a rundown of what you find on the Status bar:

- **Device name:** First is the name of your Kindle Fire HD, such as Nancy's Kindle or Nancy's 2nd Kindle.

- **Notifications:** A number sometimes appears next to the name of your device to indicate that you have notifications. A *notification* is a message alerting you about a completed download or new e-mail, for example. Tap the Notifications icon to display a list of all your notifications (see Figure 2-10).

- **Current time:** The next item on the Status bar is the current time, based on the time zone you specified when you set up the Kindle Fire HD.

- **Quick Settings:** Swipe down on the Status bar to access Quick Settings. Use these items to adjust volume, brightness, or your wireless connection, for example. To access the full Settings menu, tap More to see the full list of Settings shown in Figure 2-11.

  See Chapter 3 for a detailed breakdown of all Kindle Fire HD settings.

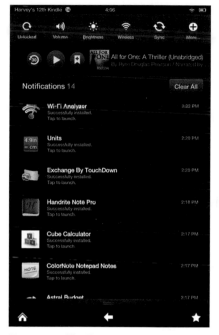

Figure 2-10: The list of current notifications that you can display from any screen.

✔ **Wireless Connection:** To the right of the displayed time is an icon showing you the wireless connection status. The more bars shown in the symbol, the stronger the connection.

✔ **Bluetooth:** This icon appears when Bluetooth is turned on. It displays in a grayed-out color when no Bluetooth device has been connected, and displays in a blue color when another Bluetooth device is connected.

✔ **Battery charge:** Finally, the Status bar holds an icon that indicates the level of charge remaining on your battery.

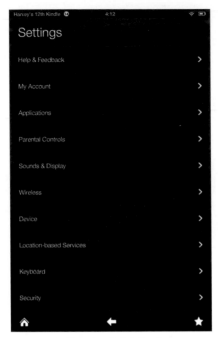

Figure 2-11: Use the Quick Settings menu or tap More to access the full complement of settings for Kindle Fire HD.

The often-present, ever-changing Options bar

The Options bar runs along the bottom or right side of your Kindle Fire HD screen, depending on which app or library you open. Items displayed here can change, again depending on what library or app you're using. Whereas the Home icon is always present, other items, such as Search and a star-shaped icon for viewing Favorites, appear often but not always. You frequently see a Menu icon when you tap the Options bar. This icon, which looks like a little box with three lines in it, makes available commonly used actions related to the screen you're viewing. Figure 2-12 shows you the options available on the Music library screen.

Figure 2-12: The Options bar offers contextually relevant options, depending on which app is displayed.

Tap Home on the Options bar to take you back to the Kindle Fire HD Home screen at any time. Some screens, such as the e-reader, keep the Options bar hidden because it would be an annoying distraction. If you don't see the Options bar, tap the bottom of the screen to make it appear.

Using a Micro-USB Cable to Transfer Data

To transfer content from your computer to the Kindle Fire HD, use the micro-USB cable that came with your Kindle Fire HD. This cable has a USB connector on one end that you can plug in +to your PC or Mac. The other end of the cable has a micro-USB connector that fits into the slot on your Kindle Fire HD.

When attached, your Kindle Fire HD should appear as a drive in Windows Explorer or the Mac Finder. Click and drag files from your hard drive to the Kindle Fire HD, or use the copy and paste functions to accomplish the same thing.

You can transfer apps, photos, documents, music, e-books, and videos from your computer to your Kindle Fire HD. Then just tap the relevant library (such as Books for e-books and Music for songs) to read or play the content on your Kindle Fire HD.

You can also upload content to your Amazon Cloud library from your computer, and that content will then be available on your Kindle Fire HD from the Cloud. See Chapter 7 for more about how this process works.

Chapter 3
Kindle Fire HD Settings

*R*ight out of the box, the Kindle Fire HD uses default settings that will work for most people most of the time. In this chapter, you look at ways to personalize these settings and make your Kindle Fire HD work uniquely for you.

Dozens of settings are available to help you manage your tablet experience. We tell you about some of these settings in the chapters that cover individual features, such as the Amazon video player (Chapter 8) and Contacts (Chapter 9). This chapter covers the more general settings.

Opening Quick Settings

You access both a short list of commonly used settings and all the more detailed settings for the Kindle Fire HD by dragging downward from the top of the screen.

Here are the settings that you can control from the Quick Settings menu (see Figure 3-1):

Figure 3-1: Quick Settings control the settings that you access most often.

✔ **Unlocked/Lock:** This is a toggle feature, meaning that you tap it to lock or unlock the automatic screen rotation for your device.

✔ **Volume:** Tap Volume to display a slider bar that you can use to increase or decrease the volume.

✔ **Brightness:** Tap to display Automatic Brightness On/Off buttons to set a feature that controls the brightness of the screen based on ambient light. You can also use the slider beneath this setting (see Figure 3-2) to adjust the brightness manually.

Figure 3-2: Adjust brightness manually by using this slider.

✔ **Wireless:** Tap to display an On/Off button (see Figure 3-3) that you can use to put the device in Airplane Mode. When Airplane Mode is on, all wireless features are turned off — including Bluetooth, Wi-Fi, and (in the case of the 4G LTE model), 4G cellular. You can also independently turn on or off each of the wireless features — Bluetooth, Wi-Fi, and 4G LTE — separately on this screen. When Wi-Fi is turned on, a list of available networks appears. Tap an available network to join it. Note that you may be asked to enter a password to access some networks.

✔ **Sync:** When you're within range of a wireless network, content downloads automatically and very quickly. However, if you've been out of range of a wireless network and have purchased new content from a computer, you can use this setting when you're back in range to manually initiate the download of that new content.

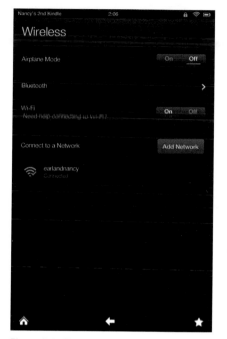

Figure 3-3: Choose from the list of available networks.

Finding Other Settings

There is one more item on the Quick Settings menu — More. Figure 3-4 shows you the many settings that appear when you tap the More button.

You won't need to change many of these settings very often. But just in case you do want to modify some settings, such as keyboard settings or parental controls, the following sections give you the skinny on what settings appear when you tap More in the Quick Settings menu.

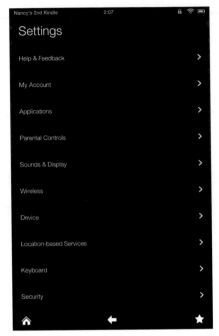

Nancy's 2nd Kindle	2:07	🔒 📶 🔋
Settings		
Help & Feedback		>
My Account		>
Applications		>
Parental Controls		>
Sounds & Display		>
Wireless		>
Device		>
Location-based Services		>
Keyboard		>
Security		>

Figure 3-4: Plenty more settings are revealed when you tap More.

Help & Feedback

Tap "Help & Feedback" from Settings to see a world of help and a way for you to interact with Amazon customer service (see Figure 3-5).

Here's what these options provide:

- ✔ **Getting Started:** Use this feature to get help with the following topics: Your Kindle, at a Glance; Connecting Wirelessly; Set Up Your Kindle; and Kindle Support Pages.

- ✔ **User Guide:** The User Guide provides a more comprehensive set of information on topics including Navigation, Shop, Games, Web, and Video Chat, among others.

- ✔ **Customer Service:** Use the Select an Issue drop-down list to locate and tap a particular issue. Then tap the Select Issue Details drop-down list that appears to choose a more specific topic. Tap E-mail or Phone to select the How Would You Like to Contact Us option.

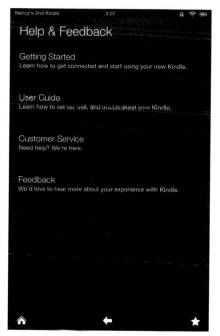

Figure 3-5: Help & Feedback settings for the Kindle Fire HD.

> ✔ **Feedback:** Tap Select a Feature and choose from the list
> that appears. Enter your comment in the Tell Us What
> You Think about This Feature field. You can also tap one
> to five stars to rate the feature. Tap the Send Feedback
> button to submit your thoughts to Amazon.

My Account

Kindle Fire HD does much of what it does by accessing your
Amazon account — to shop, access your Amazon Cloud
library online, and register your Kindle Fire HD, for example.

The My Account option in Settings provides information
about the registered account (see Figure 3-6). Your Kindle
e-mail address is displayed, which you can use to send personal
documents to your Kindle. To remove the account from your
Kindle Fire HD, tap the Deregister button. You are then
presented with a Register button. Tap Register and fill in your
Amazon username and password to register the device.

Figure 3-6: Check which Amazon account your device is registered to.

If you deregister your account, you once again see the introductory demo that appeared when you first set up your Kindle Fire HD. When you finish that demo and tap any category, such as Books, you're again prompted to register your device to your Amazon account.

The My Account screen also offers the option of managing social networking accounts and e-mail accounts. Use the former to set up your Twitter or Facebook account so that you can take advantage of built-in features for sharing information via either service. Tap the e-mail link to manage general e-mail settings.

Parental Controls

Tap the On button to set parental controls. You then enter a password, confirm it, and then tap Finish.

In the screen shown in Figure 3-7, tap to block or unblock the Web Browser or E-mail, Contacts, Calendars settings. You can also tap to password-protect purchases or video playback. If you want to allow or block certain types of content, tap Block and Unblock Content Types, and then tap to block the specific content you want to block.

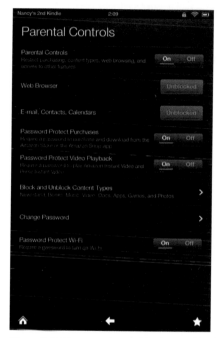

Figure 3-7: Choose what to block or unblock here.

You can also tap to turn on or off the feature to password-protect Wi-Fi. With this setting on, anybody using your Kindle Fire HD has to enter a password to make an online connection.

Controlling sounds and display

If you tap Sounds & Display in Kindle Settings, you see a volume slider that you can use to move the volume up or down as well as a setting for turning Dolby Digital Plus on or off. The Dolby setting improves the Kindle Fire HD's sound quality but may use up slightly more of your battery life.

You also see two settings controlling Notification Sounds. Notifications may come from the arrival of a new e-mail, a completed download, or an app notification. To modify Notification Sounds, tap to Mute All Notifications, or tap the check box arrow on the right of Notification Sounds. From the list that appears, you can choose the sound you want to use.

You can also manage your device's display, adjusting both the screen brightness and screen timeout, which sets how long it takes for the screen to lock when the device isn't being used.

Location-Based Services

New with Kindle Fire HD is a location-based feature that enables the device to know where you are. This capability is useful for apps and features that need to know where you are to provide information or services, such as weather or local traffic reports. When an app or website is using your location information, you see an icon that looks like a cross in a circle in the upper-right corner near your battery life icon.

To turn Location-Based Services on or off, from the Settings screen, tap Location-Based Services and then tap the On/Off button.

Creating security settings

The first thing you can do to keep your Kindle Fire HD secure is to never let it out of your hands. But because we can't control everything and sometimes things get lost or stolen, it's a good idea to assign a password that's required to unlock your Kindle Fire HD screen. That way, if someone gets his hands on your Kindle Fire HD, he has no way to get at your Amazon account information or contacts.

Tap the Security Settings option to see four choices:

✓ **Lock Screen Password On/Off:** Tap On, and fields appear labeled Enter Password and Confirm Password. Tap in the Enter Password field and, using the onscreen keyboard that appears, type a password. Tap in the Confirm Password field and retype the password. Tap Finish to save your new password.

✔ **Credential Storage:** Credentials are typically used for secure access to Microsoft Exchange–based accounts, such as an account that you use to access e-mail on your company's server. If you use Microsoft Exchange, it's a good idea to get your network administrator's help to put these settings in place.

✔ **VPN:** To connect the Kindle Fire HD to a virtual private network, you first use this feature to download a VPN app from the Appstore.

Device Administrators: If your device is being administered through a company Exchange account, use this setting to establish the device administrator who can modify settings for the account.

✔ **Enable ADB:** This setting allows people who are developing apps for Kindle Fire HD to run debugging programs using a USB connection. The average consumer doesn't need to worry about this setting.

Working with applications

When you tap Applications in Settings, you see several options followed by a list of your installed apps.

Tap Installed Applications in the screen shown in Figure 3-8; then tap any of the installed apps such as a Calendar or Amazon Kindle and you encounter the following options:

✔ **Force Stop:** Force Stop allows Kindle Fire HD to stop an application if it encounters problems.

✔ **Storage:** You can clear the Kindle Fire HD's memory of data stored by the app by tapping the Clear Data button.

✔ **Cache:** Computing devices store data based on your usage to more quickly provide the data you need. This so-called cache of data fills up a bit of memory, so if you want to free up some memory, tap the Clear Cache button.

✔ **Launch by Default:** Not all apps will have this setting. Tap this button to launch an app automatically when you turn on Kindle Fire HD if that option is available.

✔ **Permissions:** This is a list of permissions to allow access to information that this app might have to use to perform its function, such as your location.

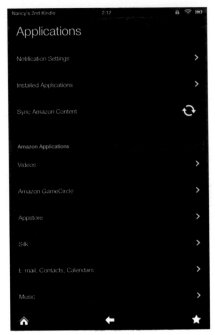

Figure 3-8: Each application on your Kindle Fire HD has associated settings.

Setting up Wireless

Wireless is a pretty essential setting for using Kindle Fire HD. Without a wireless connection, you can't stream video or music, shop at the various Amazon stores, or send and receive e-mail.

- ✔ **Airplane Mode:** Although this sounds confusing, when set to On, this setting turns off all your device's wireless communications: Bluetooth, Wi-Fi, and (if applicable) 4G LTE. You'll want to turn Airplane Mode on when you're on an airplane, where wireless signals are not allowed. Also, in Airplane Mode, your battery charge will last somewhat longer.

- ✔ **Bluetooth:** Settings here allow you to connect to a Bluetooth device, such as a Bluetooth printer or cell phone.

- ✔ **Wi-Fi:** Tap the On/Off button to turn Wi-Fi on or off. Note that turning Wi-Fi off may extend your Kindle Fire HD's battery charge.

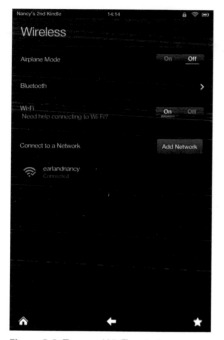

Figure 3-9: Turn on Wi-Fi and choose your preferred Wi-Fi network.

🖙 **Connect to a Network:** Tap the Add Network button included with this setting to enter a new network's SSID (the public name of a Wi-Fi network).

🖙 **Connect to a Network:** Tap any network listed here to connect to it. If you are in range of a network that isn't listed here, tap the Add Network button and enter its SSID to connect to it.

Working with the keyboard

No physical keyboard comes with your Kindle Fire HD, so you depend on its onscreen keyboard to provide input to apps such as Quickoffice, or into fields used to search and enter text into forms, such as e-mail messages.

You can do five simple things with Kindle Keyboard settings, three of which offer the basic On/Off choices (see Figure 3-10):

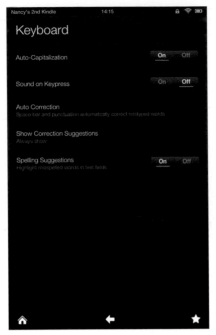

Figure 3-10: Control your onscreen keyboard with these settings.

- ✓ **Auto-Capitalization:** If you want Kindle Fire HD to automatically capitalize proper names or the first word in a sentence, tap to turn this setting on.

- ✓ **Sound on Keypress:** If you like that satisfying clicky sound when you tap a keyboard key, tap to turn this setting on.

- ✓ **Auto Correction:** Turning this setting on allows Kindle Fire HD to correct common typing errors, such as typing *teh* when you mean *the.*

- ✓ **Show Correction Suggestions:** You can choose to always show correction suggestions, show them only when you're holding your Kindle Fire HD in portrait orientation, or always hide them.

- ✓ **Spelling Suggestions:** Turn this feature on to highlight potentially misspelled words in text fields.

Looking at device settings

You can check your Kindle Fire HD's device settings (see Figure 3-11) to find out facts such as the remaining storage

space available or your device's serial number and to reset
your Kindle to its initial out-of-the-box state.

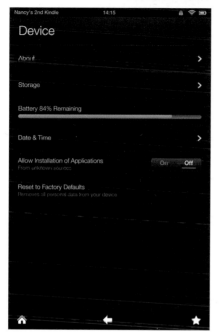

Figure 3-11: Device settings provide a lot of information about the status of your device.

Here are the device settings available to you:

- ✔ **About:** Reveals system information such as your current System Version (also known as firmware).

- ✔ **Storage:** Tells you how much memory is still available on your device.

- ✔ **Battery:** Indicates the percentage of battery power remaining.

- ✔ **Date and Time:** Creates settings for your time zone.

- ✔ **Allow Installation of Applications:** The Kindle Fire HD is set up to get its content from Amazon because that source provides some measure of confidence and security. Apps that you transfer from your computer to Kindle Fire HD that are from third-party suppliers are more likely to introduce viruses to your computer. Still, you can buy apps elsewhere and port them over from your computer. If you want to allow this capability, choose On in this setting.

✔ **Reset to Factory Defaults:** This setting is not something you want to choose accidentally! This setting could come in handy, though, if you give or sell your Kindle Fire HD to somebody and don't want that person to have your account information. This setting wipes all content from the device and any changes you've made to default settings. If you tap this setting, you see the confirming dialog box shown in Figure 3-12. Tap Erase Everything to continue with the reset procedure or Cancel to close the warning dialog box and halt the reset.

Figure 3-12: Be sure that you want to reset before you accept this option.

Although you get a minimum of 16GB or 32GB of storage with the Kindle Fire HD, a chunk of that is taken up in pre-installed and system files. So the storage available may indicate that you have less total storage available on the device than you thought.

Chapter 4
Going Shopping

*K*indle Fire HD is a great device for consuming content. Buying content, or downloading free content, is a key step to enjoying it. Amazon offers a rich supply of books, magazines, music, and video, as well as apps from the Amazon Appstore. In this chapter, you can discover how to get this content for your Kindle Fire HD.

Managing Your Amazon Account

To buy items directly from your Kindle Fire HD, you need to associate your Amazon account with your Kindle Fire HD. You do so during the setup process covered in Chapter 2, or you can get it done by visiting the My Account section of Settings (see Figure 4-1).

After you associate your device with an Amazon account, you can manage account settings by following these steps:

1. **Go to the Amazon website (**www.amazon.com**) using the browser on your Kindle Fire HD (or your computer browser).**

2. **Tap (or click) Your Account at the top right of the Amazon screen (see Figure 4-2).**

3. Tap (or click, on your computer) **Manage Payment Options** or **Add a Credit or Debit Card** from the Payment section of your account.

4. Change or enter a new method of payment and billing address.

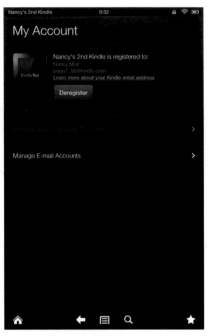

Figure 4-1: Swipe down on the top of your screen, tap More, and then choose My Account in the Settings page to view this screen.

Figure 4-2: Managing your Amazon account on a PC.

Visiting the Amazon Appstore

Now you can shop for all kinds of content from your Kindle Fire HD. I start by introducing you to the world of apps.

Apps provide you with functionality of all kinds: star gazing, playing games, drawing, using maps, and thousands of other fun and useful kinds.

Exploring the world of apps

The Amazon Appstore is full of apps written especially for devices that are based on the Android platform, including the Kindle Fire HD.

 Android devices may have slightly different operating systems, therefore not every app will work on every device. See Chapters 11 and 12 for some suggested apps that work well with your Kindle Fire HD.

To explore the world of apps, tap Apps at the top of your Home screen and then tap Store from the Apps library. The store shown in Figure 4-3 appears.

 At the top of the store is Today's Free App of the Day. You can get a different free app every day; just be sure not to glut your Kindle Fire HD's memory with free apps that you're not really going to use.

Above the free app offer are the following options:

- **Best Sellers:** Tap this to display the best selling apps in the store, including Top Paid, Top Free, and Top Rated.

- **Games:** Tap Games to see featured game titles. Across the top of the Games section of the store are links such as Action, Arcade, Casual, Puzzles, and All Games.

- **New Releases:** Tap this to see recent releases across a variety of categories — a great way to browse new additions since your last app shopping spree.

- **All Categories**: Tap All Categories to access all app categories ranging from City Info to Cooking to Real Estate and Travel (see Figure 4-4).

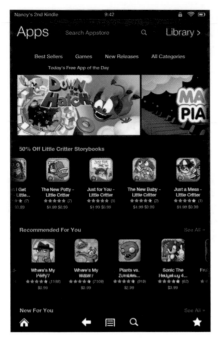

Figure 4-3: The Amazon Appstore.

 When you display a category of apps, note that you can tap the Refine button to sort the apps by the following categories: Relevance, New Releases, Average Customer Review, or Price.

Searching for apps

If you know which app you want to buy, using the search feature can take you right to it if you follow these steps:

1. **Tap in the Search Appstore field on the Appstore main page.**

   The keyboard shown in Figure 4-5 appears.

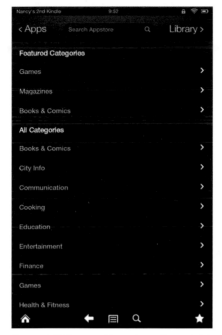

Figure 4-4: See a wide variety of special-interest apps by tapping All Categories.

2. **Using the onscreen keyboard, enter the name of an app, such as Angry Birds (which is a game).**

   Suggestions appear beneath the Search field.

3. **Tap a suggestion to display the list of suggestions with more detailed results, as shown in Figure 4-5.**

4. **Tap an app name to see more details about it.**

   Product Info appears, as shown in Figure 4-6, with screenshots, a description, and customer reviews.

The Save for Later button adds the app to your Saved list. You access this list by tapping the Menu button on the Options bar, tapping More, and then tapping Saved for Later.

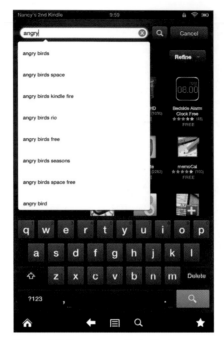

Figure 4-5: Search results in the Appstore.

Buying apps

When you're ready to buy, you can follow these steps:

1. **From the product description, tap the Price button.**

   This button displays the price or FREE. When you tap the button, its label changes to Get App.

2. **Tap the button again to have the app downloaded to your Kindle Fire HD.**

   A Downloading graphic appears, showing the download progress. When the download is complete, an Open button appears.

3. **Tap the Open button to use the app immediately.**

To use the app later, locate it and tap it in the App library or, if you've used it recently, on the Carousel.

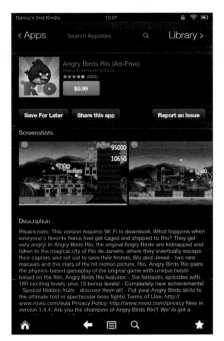

Figure 4-6: Product details are shown in the Product Info screen.

 You can let others know about an app by using e-mail. Tap the Share This App button on the app description page in the Amazon Appstore (refer to Figure 4-3), to use this feature.

Note: In doing so, you're not really sharing the ability to use the app. The Share This App feature just enables you to easily let others know about a particular app.

 You can also buy apps from the Appstore on your PC or Mac. Select Kindle Fire HD for the device you want to download the app to in the drop-down list below the Add to Cart button. The app is immediately downloaded to your Kindle Fire HD.

To delete an installed app, press and hold its icon until a menu appears. (The icon is the graphical image of the app that appears in your Apps library or your Carousel.) On that menu, tap Remove from Device. The app isn't completely gone from your grasp, however. It's still stored in the Cloud, where you can download it again at any time by tapping Cloud in the App library and then tapping the app.

Buying Content

Shopping for content is our favorite thing to do with our Kindle Fire HD. Content means an evening with a movie, a rainy afternoon with a good book, or a relaxing hour listening to a soothing collection of music.

From Amazon, you can buy publications, books, music, and video to download or stream to your Kindle Fire HD.

Buying publications through Newsstand

A wide selection of magazines and newspapers is waiting for you to explore! The Kindle Fire HD's color display makes browsing through color magazines especially appealing.

Tap Newsstand on the Home page of the Kindle Fire HD; then tap Store to see several categories of items (see Figure 4-7).

Figure 4-7: The Newsstand store.

Featured Magazines with 30-day free trials are displayed across the top. Swipe right or left to scroll through these items.

Below Free Trials, you see categories such as Best Sellers, Business & Investing, and Entertaining. (The displayed categories change on a regular basis.)

Tap See All above any category to see a more complete list of included items.

When you find the publication you want, follow these steps to buy or subscribe to it:

1. **Tap the item.**

   A screen appears, showing pricing, a description of the publication, and Subscribe Now and Buy Issue buttons (see Figure 4-8). If an issue is available for free, you see a Free button instead.

Figure 4-8: This screen shows details about a publication and buttons to help you purchase or subscribe.

2. **Tap Subscribe Now or Buy Issue.**

   The button label changes to display Downloading; it then displays Read Now when the download is complete.

3. **Tap the Read Now button to open the magazine.**

   Note that the magazine is stored in your Amazon Cloud library, where you can read or download it to your Kindle Fire HD via Newsstand at a later time.

Buying books

You'll find that reading books on Kindle Fire HD is convenient and economical. To browse through an e-book, follow these steps:

1. **Tap Books on the Kindle Fire HD Home screen.**

2. **Tap Store.**

   The Amazon Books store sports a Recommended for You section at the top, recommending books based on your buying history.

3. **Swipe right to left to scroll horizontally through recommendations at the top.**

   You also see categories such as Kindle Select 25, Best Sellers, and Editor's Picks.

4. **Tap a book cover to get more information for that book.**

   You see a screen with that item's pricing and description (see Figure 4-9).

The buttons you see at this point are labeled Try a Sample, Add to Wish List, and Buy (or Buy for Free). Here's how these two buttons work:

   ✔ **Try A Sample:** Tap this button and it changes first to a Downloading button and then, when downloading is complete, to a Read Now button. Tap the Read Now button to open the sample of the book.

Figure 4-9: Details about a book in the Amazon Books store.

> 🖊 **Buy or Buy for Free:** Tap this button and it changes to a Downloading button. When the download is complete, the button label changes to Read Now. Tap the Read Now button to open the book. If you purchased the book by accident, you can press the Cancel Order link.

After you've read a bit of your new book, it will appear both in your Books library and on the Carousel on the Home screen.

To remove a book from your device, open your Books library, press and hold the book, and tap Remove from Device from the menu that appears.

For more about reading e-books and periodicals on the Kindle Fire HD, see Chapter 6.

Buying music

You may hate computer games and you might not read books very often, but I've never met anybody who doesn't like some kind of music. No matter what kind of music you prefer, from hip-hop to Broadway, you're likely to find a great many selections tucked away in Amazon's vaults.

Tap Music on the Kindle Fire HD Home screen and then tap Store. On the right side of the Store screen, you see the following categories: Bestsellers, New Releases, and Genres. Tap one of these to get a list of items in that category (see Figure 4-10). You can also tap categories such as New Releases and Recommended for You to view music by these criteria.

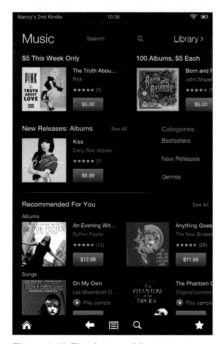

Figure 4-10: The Amazon Music store.

All over the Music store home page, you see thumbnails of music selections.

Follow these steps to buy music:

1. **Tap an item.**

   A screen appears, displaying a list of the songs in the case of an album with Price buttons for both the entire album and each individual song.

2. **Tap the arrow button to the left of a song to play a preview of it.**

3. **Tap a Price button.**

   The button label changes from the price of the item to the word Buy.

4. **Tap the Buy button.**

   The song or album downloads to your Music library. A confirmation dialog box opens, displaying a Go to Your Library button and a Continue Shopping button.

5. **Tap the Go to Your Library button to open the album and display the list of songs.**

   The album is now stored both in your Music library and the Cloud; if you tap a song to play it, it'll also appear with recently accessed content in the Carousel. The first time you download music, you may be asked to choose whether you want content downloaded to your device or stored in the Amazon Cloud when you buy it.

   If you tap the Continue Shopping button, you can later find the album in your Music library.

See Chapter 7 for more about playing music.

Buying video

You should definitely check out the experience of consuming your video programs on a portable device such as the Kindle Fire HD. From lying in bed or on the beach to watching your videos while waiting in line at the bank, portability can be a very convenient feature.

When you tap Videos on the Kindle Fire HD Home screen, you're instantly taken to the Amazon Video store, shown in Figure 4-11.

Figure 4-11: Shop for video in the Amazon Video store.

Thumbnails of items are displayed in the Prime Instant Videos category. Beneath these thumbnails is a horizontally scrolling list of thumbnails for movies you've bought previously, labeled Next Up. You can pick up where you left off viewing these items by tapping any of them.

Tap an item in the Prime Instant Video category. For TV shows, a screen appears with episode prices and a set of Season tabs. For movies, this screen may include Watch Trailer, Buy, and Rent buttons. You can also scroll down and view details such as the movie's director and release year.

Tap a Price button and the button becomes a Rent or Buy button. Tap this button and your purchase or rental is processed.

Tap a Rent button for movies and you see a Rent or Rent HD button. Tap one of these and you're immediately charged for the rental. The rental period begins when you start to watch the movie.

See Chapter 8 for more about playing videos.

 Tap the Watchlist button to add the item to your watchlist so that you can go back and rent or buy it at some future time. To view your Watchlist, tap the menu button on the Options bar when in the Videos library or store; then tap Your Watchlist.

Shopping for Anything Else

Amazon pre-installed an Amazon Shopping app on your Kindle Fire HD so that you can easily go to its online store and buy anything your heart desires.

Just tap Apps from the Kindle Fire HD home screen and then tap the Shop Amazon app. Amazon opens in your browser with a list of recommendations for you, based on previous purchases. You can tap the Shop by Departments button to access a drop-down list of available departments.

Now, just proceed to shop as you usually do on Amazon, tapping any item of interest to add it to your cart.

Chapter 5
Going Online

*K*indle Fire HD can become your new go-to device for keeping informed and in touch by using Amazon's Silk browser and the pre-installed e-mail client.

In this chapter, you discover the ins and outs of browsing with Silk and the simple tools you can use to send and receive e-mail on the Kindle Fire HD.

Browsing with Silk

Silk is the browser that takes advantage of Amazon's ability to use its own servers to make your browsing experience speedy. The browser is designed to make your browsing experience as fast and smooth as, well, silk!

Many of Silk's tools and features will be familiar to you from other browsers, but a few are unique to Silk.

Using navigation tools to get around

From the Kindle Fire HD Home screen, tap Web in the list displayed across the top of the screen to see Silk, shown in Figure 5-1.

Address/Search field

Bookmarks button   Add button

Back button   Menu button

Forward button

Figure 5-1: Silk offers a familiar browser interface.

You can use the Back and Forward buttons to move among pages you've previously viewed. To go directly to a page, tap in the Address field (note that this field will act as a Search field if you enter a word or phrase, or as an Address field if you enter a website's address, or URL). Tap in the field, enter a site address using the onscreen keyboard, and tap Enter. The website is displayed.

Silk uses tabs that allow you to display more than one web page at a time and move among those pages. Tap the Add button — which features a plus sign (+) — to add a tab in the browser. When you do, thumbnails of recently visited sites appear. You can tap a thumbnail to go to that site, or you can tap in the Address bar and enter a URL by using the onscreen keyboard.

Bookmarking sites

You can bookmark sites in Silk so that you can easily jump back to those sites again. With a site displayed onscreen, tap the Bookmark icon to the left of the Address bar to easily add a bookmark for that site.

Another way to add a bookmark is to tap the Add button and then tap Bookmarks. In the Add Bookmark dialog box that appears (see Figure 5-2), tap OK to bookmark the currently displayed page. You can then tap the Add button shown in Figure 5-2 and tap Bookmarks to display thumbnails of all bookmarked pages. Tap one to go there.

Figure 5-2: Bookmarks help you quickly return to a favorite page.

To delete a bookmark, after tapping the Bookmarks button to display thumbnails of bookmarked pages, press and hold a page. In the menu that appears, tap Delete. In the confirming dialog box that appears, tap OK and the bookmark is removed.

When a website is open in Silk, the Menu button on the Options bar also provides a Share Page feature. When you tap this option, you can select to share the current page via e-mail.

Searching for content on a page

Web pages can contain a lot of content, so it's not always easy to find the article or discussion you want to view on a particular topic. Most browsers provide a feature to search for content on a web page, and Silk is no exception.

To search the currently displayed page by using Silk, follow these steps:

1. **Tap Menu on the Options bar.**

2. **On the screen that appears, tap Find in Page.**

   The onscreen keyboard appears with the Search field active.

3. **Type a search term.**

   The search term appears in an orange highlight on the first instance of that word on the page. Other instances of that word on the page are highlighted, as shown in Figure 5-3 (and appear in yellow on your device).

4. **Tap Done to end the search.**

Searching the web

Most of us spend a lot of our time online browsing around to find what we want. Search engines make our lives easier because they help us narrow down what we're looking for by using specific search terms.

To search the entire web, follow these steps:

1. **Tap the plus sign (+) to add a tab in the browser if you want search results to appear on a new tab.**

   Thumbnails of recently visited sites appear.

Figure 5-3: The first instance of a word on a page is indicated by an orange highlight.

2. **Tap in the Search field.**

   The thumbnails change to a list of bookmarked sites, and the onscreen keyboard appears.

3. **Enter a Search term and tap Go.**

   As you enter the first few letters of the search term, suggested search terms appear below the Search field (see Figure 5-4). When you tap Go, results appear in your default search engine.

4. **Tap a result to go to that page.**

To specify a search engine to use other than the default, tap the Menu button in the Options bar and then tap Settings. Tap Search Engine option to choose Bing, Google, or Yahoo! as the default search engine.

Figure 5-4: Suggestions are displayed as you type your search term.

Reviewing browsing history

You can review your browsing history to see what sites you visited recently.

With Silk open, tap the Add button. Tap History, and sites you've visited on the Kindle Fire HD appear in a list divided into categories such as Today and Last 7 Days. When you find the name of the one you want, tap it to go there.

To avoid losing a site that you know you want to revisit, bookmark it as described in the earlier section, "Bookmarking sites."

Working with web page content

Sometimes you may find online content, such as a PDF file, that you want to download to your Docs library. Or maybe you've found an image that you want to download to the

Photos library on your device. You can also open or share content you find online. Here's how these work:

- ✓ **View downloads.** Tap Menu on the Options bar and then tap the Downloads button that appears to view completed downloads.

- ✓ **Save or view images.** Press and hold an image. A menu appears, offering options such as Save Image or View Image (see Figure 5-5).

- ✓ **Work with links.** Press and hold your finger on any linked text. A menu appears with options, including Open, Open in New Tab, Open in Background Tab, Bookmark Link, Save Link, Share Link, and Copy Link URL.

Figure 5-5: You can work with links and images by using this menu.

You can download and use a different browser if you like. Tap Apps on the Home screen, tap Store, and then type **browser** in the Search box. Tap on the browser you prefer to use, such as Chrome or Firefox, and download the free or at-a-cost browser to your Kindle Fire.

Personalizing Silk

Silk sports a nice, clean interface. Still, you can do a few things to personalize the way Silk looks and acts and make it work better for you.

With Silk open, tap the Menu button on the Options bar and then tap Settings. A screen appears (see Figure 5-6), showing some of the options you can use to control the Silk browser's behavior. Swipe your finger down to see all the options available, including the following:

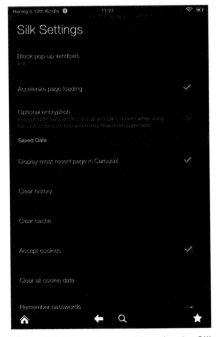

Figure 5-6: The various settings for the Silk browser.

- ✔ **Block Pop-up Windows:** Require Silk to ask about displaying pop-up windows; never display them; or always display them.

- ✔ **Display Most Recent Page in Carousel:** Specify whether recently visited web pages are displayed in the Carousel.

You can double-tap a page to enlarge the view and double-tap again to reduce the view. Or place your fingers pinched together on the screen and then spread them out to enlarge the view. To reduce the view size, start with your fingers spread apart and then pinch them together.

✒ **Remember Passwords:** This option saves you the time of entering usernames and passwords for sites you visit often. Just be aware that this setting puts your accounts at risk should you ever misplace your Kindle Fire HD.

If you want to get rid of all the settings you've made to Silk, make sure that you have Silk open. On the Options bar, tap the Menu button and then Settings. Scroll down to Advanced Settings and then tap Reset All Settings to Default.

Working with E-Mail

The Kindle Fire HD has a built-in e-mail client. A *client* essentially allows you to access e-mail accounts that you've set up through various providers, such as Gmail and Windows Live Hotmail. You can then open the inboxes of these accounts and read, reply to, and forward messages by using your Kindle Fire HD. You can also create and send new messages, and even include attachments.

In the following sections, we provide information about setting up and using your e-mail accounts on the Kindle Fire HD.

Setting up an e-mail account

Setting up your e-mail on the Kindle Fire HD involves providing information about one or more e-mail accounts that you've already established with a provider such as Gmail.

Follow these steps to set up an e-mail account the first time you use the app:

1. **Drag from the top of the screen to display Settings.**

   The Quick Settings appear.

2. **Tap More.**

   The Settings panel appears.

3. **Tap My Account.**

4. **Tap Manage E-mail Accounts.**

5. **Tap Add Account.**

   The dialog box shown in Figure 5-7 appears.

6. **Tap AOL, Exchange, Gmail, Hotmail, Yahoo, or Other Provider.**

7. **Enter your username, e-mail address, and password in the appropriate fields and then tap Next.**

   A new screen appears, displaying two fields.

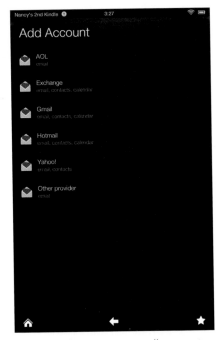

Figure 5-7: Choose your e-mail account.

8. **Enter the name that will appear on outgoing messages in the Name field and an address in the E-mail Address field for your e-mail account.**

   The account name is optional.

9. Enter the password for your e-mail account in the Password field.

10. Tap the Send Mail from This Account by Default check box if you want to set this up as your default e-mail account; then tap Next.

11. If a message appears about how some accounts sync with your Kindle Fire, tap OK to proceed. In the final screen, tap Save. Tap the View Inbox button to go to the inbox for the account you just set up.

You can set up as many e-mail accounts as you like. When you open the Kindle Fire HD Email app, you see a Unified Inbox that combines messages from all accounts you set up. You also see individual inboxes for each account.

Sending e-mail

After you set up your e-mail account(s), as described in the preceding section, you're able to send e-mails from your Kindle Fire HD. To create and send an e-mail, with the Email app and an e-mail account inbox open, follow these steps:

1. Tap the New button.

   A blank e-mail form appears, as shown in Figure 5-8.

2. In the To field, enter a name.

   Alternatively, tap the Add Contacts button, which features a plus sign (+), to open the Contacts app and tap a name there to add that person as an addressee.

3. If you want to send a copy of the e-mail to somebody, tap the Options button to make those fields appear; then enter addresses or choose them from the Contacts app by tapping the Add Contacts button.

4. Tap in the Subject field and enter a subject by using the onscreen keyboard.

5. Tap in the Message text field and enter a message.

6. (Optional) If you want to add an attachment to an e-mail, tap the Attach button shown to the right of the Cc field and, in the menu that appears, choose to attach an item from the Photos app, OfficeSuite, or Personal Videos.

Figure 5-8: A blank form waiting for you to enter an e-mail address, subject, and message.

7. **To send your message, tap the Send button at the bottom of the screen.**

   If you decide that you're not ready to send the message quite yet, you also have the option of tapping the Cancel button and then tapping Save Draft.

Here are a couple of handy shortcuts for entering text in your e-mail. First is the Auto Complete feature, which lists possible word matches as you type; tap one to complete a word. In addition, you can double-tap to place a period and space at the end of a sentence.

Receiving e-mail

The Kindle Fire HD can receive your e-mail messages whenever you're connected to a Wi-Fi network.

When an e-mail is delivered to your inbox (see Figure 5-9), simply tap to open it. Read it and contemplate whether you want to save it or delete it (or forward or reply to it, as covered in the following section). If you don't need to keep the message, you can delete it by tapping the Delete button at the top of the screen.

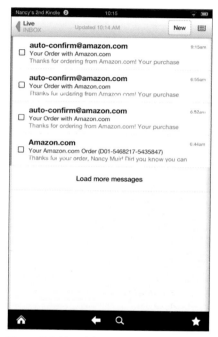

Figure 5-9: Your inbox.

If you're expecting an e-mail but don't see it in your inbox, try tapping the Menu button in the top-right corner and tapping Refresh. Doing so pulls any new e-mails into your inbox.

Forwarding and replying to e-mail

When you receive an e-mail, you can choose to reply to the sender, reply to the sender and anybody else who was included as an addressee on the original message, or forward the e-mail to another person.

If you reply to all recipients, you send an answer to the sender, anybody else in the To field of the original message, and anybody in the Cc and Bcc fields. Because Bcc fields aren't visible to you as a recipient, you may be sending your reply to people you're not aware of.

To forward or reply to an e-mail, with the Email app inbox displayed, follow these steps:

1. **Tap an e-mail to open it.**

2. **Tap the Respond button.**

   A menu of options appears.

3. **Tap Reply, Reply All, or Forward.**

4. **If you're forwarding the message, enter a new recipient.**

   If you're replying, the message is already addressed, but you can enter additional recipients if you want.

5. **Tap in the message area and enter your message.**

6. **Tap the Send button to send your message on its way.**

When you read a message, it is marked as read when the sender's name no longer appears in bold. To mark it as unread again (if, for example, you want to draw your attention to it so that you know to read it again), tap the box to the left of the e-mail in your inbox and then tap the Mark button in the top-right corner. To delete an e-mail from your inbox, select it and tap the Delete button.

Sending E-Mail to Your Kindle Account

When you register your Kindle Fire HD, you get an associated e-mail account, which essentially allows you or others to e-mail documents in Word, PDF, RTF, or HTML format to your Kindle Fire HD.

The address of the account is displayed in the Docs library. Tap the Docs Library button on the Home screen and then tap the Cloud button; you see a line that reads Send Documents to *YourE-MailAccount@kindle.com*, where *Your E-Mail Account* is the name of your Kindle e-mail account.

You or others can e-mail documents to this address, and those documents automatically appear in your Docs library. Note that you might need to go to Amazon by using a browser and change the approved e-mail accounts. Click Your Account and then Manage Your Kindle under the Digital Content section. Click the Personal Document Settings link on the left side of the screen, and make sure that the account is listed under Send to Kindle Email Settings as approved.

Chapter 6
E-Reader Extraordinaire

*T*he Kindle Fire HD comes from a family of e-readers, so it's only natural that the e-reader you use to read books and magazines on the device is a very robust feature. With its bright, colorful screen, the Kindle Fire HD broadens your reading experience beyond black-and-white books to color publications such as magazines or graphic novels. Its easy-to-use controls help you navigate publications, bookmark and highlight text, and search your libraries of print content.

In this chapter, you can discover what's available, how to open publications, and how to read and then delete them from the Kindle Fire HD when you're done.

So Many Things to Read!

Amazon started as an online book retailer, although through the years it has branched out to become the largest retailer of just about everything on the planet. The Kindle Fire HD makes it easy for you to buy your content from Amazon.

The content you buy from Amazon is automatically down-loaded to your Kindle device. In addition, you can borrow Kindle versions of books from the Amazon Lending Library as well as from many public libraries. You can also lend books to your friends.

You can buy the current issues of magazines and newspapers, and have issues delivered to your Kindle Fire HD automatically as they become available.

Buying books

To buy books for your Kindle Fire HD, on the Home screen, tap Books.

Tapping Store takes you to Amazon's Books store, shown in Figure 6-1. See Chapter 4 for more about how to search for and buy content.

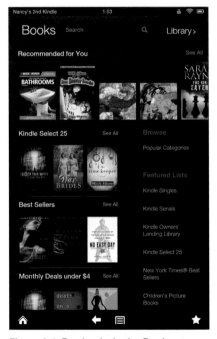

Figure 6-1: Buy books in the Books store.

You can also buy content at the Amazon website from your computer and have it downloaded to your Kindle Fire HD. Just select what device you want it delivered to from the drop-down list below the Add to Cart button.

Amazon uses a technology called Whispersync to download content to your devices. All Kindle Fire devices but the 8.9-inch 4G LTE model of the Kindle Fire HD use a Wi-Fi connection, so you need to be connected to a Wi-Fi hotspot to download publications.

Using the Amazon Lending Library

On the screen that appears when you enter the Amazon store, you see a Kindle Owner's Lending Library link on the right side of the page. Tap this and a list of free lending selections appears (see Figure 6-2). Note that these items are available for free only if you have a Prime membership.

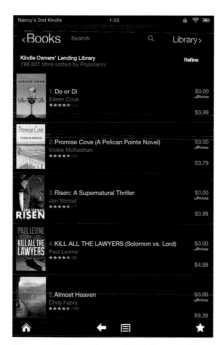

Figure 6-2: If you have the Prime service, these selections are free.

Tap an item and a descriptive page appears. Here you can tap the Borrow for Free button and your selection is immediately downloaded. You can borrow a title from the Lending Library approximately every two weeks.

Borrowing from your local library

More than 11,000 libraries in the U.S. lend Kindle versions of books through a system called Overdrive, which allows you to easily download books to your Kindle Fire HD. The length of time you can borrow a book varies by library, and each library may have a slightly different system for borrowing books. When you next try to borrow a book, if you still have one taken out of the library, a notice appears that you have to return that one before you can borrow another. Tap the Return Book button to return a book.

Here are the typical steps for borrowing Kindle books from your library, but you should ask your library for the steps that work with its system:

1. **Go to your library's website and search for eBooks.**

   Note that you'll need a library card and PIN to borrow books.

2. **Click the title that you want to check out; then enter your library card information and PIN.**

3. **After you check out a title, choose Get for Kindle.**

   You may then have to enter your Amazon.com account information to borrow the title.

4. **Choose the title and the device you want the book delivered to; then choose Get Library Book to download the title to your Kindle Fire HD.**

Lend your Kindle books to others

You can loan an e-book to anyone — even if they don't have a Kindle! All you need is the person's e-mail address.

You can loan e-books from your computer. Follow these steps to lend an e-book to a friend:

1. **Open a web browser on your personal computer and go to the Manage Your Kindle page (www.amazon. com/myk).**

   If you're not already logged in, you're prompted to do so.

2. **Scroll down to view the e-books in your Kindle library.**

3. **Hover over the Actions button for an e-book.**

   If lending has been enabled for the e-book, a Loan This Title option appears.

4. **Click the Loan This Title option, and on the page that appears, enter the person's e-mail address, name, and a message.**

   The borrower of the e-book receives an e-mail from Amazon. The borrower has seven days to accept the loan by clicking the Get Your Loaned Book Now button provided in the e-mail.

What if the person you've loaned the e-book to doesn't have a Kindle? No problem! You can use many devices to read Kindle e-books, including your computer, tablet, or mobile phone. You can download a free Kindle reading app at www.amazon.com/gp/kindle/kcp.

The borrower can return the loaned e-book before the 14-day loan is over. To return a borrowed Kindle e-book, go to the Your Orders section of the Manage Your Kindle page on Amazon. Click the plus symbol (+) next to the loaned title and then click the Delete This Title link.

 Want to know whether a book is lendable before you purchase it? From a personal computer, view the book's product page on Amazon. Scroll down to the Product Details section and look for "Lending: Enabled."

Reading Books

After you own some Kindle books, you can begin to read by using the e-reader installed on your Kindle Fire HD. In the following sections, we go over the basics of how the Kindle e-reader works.

 You can get to the Home screen from anywhere in the e-reader. If a Home button isn't visible, just tap the page to display the Options bar, which includes a Home button and a set of tools for navigating a book.

Going to the (Books) library

When you tap Books on your Kindle Fire HD screen, you open the Books library, which contains downloaded content on the Device link and content in the Cloud on the Cloud link. The active link is the one displaying orange text. You also see a Store link, which you can use to shop for books on Amazon.

Your Books library has several features that you can use to get different perspectives on its contents:

 ✔ **View by Grid and List.** Tap Menu on the Options bar to display the Grid View and List View options. These options provide views of your books by using large book covers on a bookshelf (see Figure 6-3 for the Grid view) or in a text list that includes title and author along with an accompanying small thumbnail.

 ✔ **Sort titles.** Use the By Author, By Recent, and By Title options near the top of the screen to view books by any of these three criteria.

 ✔ **Identify new titles.** If you've just downloaded but haven't started reading a book, you see a small gray banner in the corner of the thumbnail with the word New in it (see Figure 6-4).

Tap the Search button on the Options bar to search your Books library contents by title or author.

Opening a book

To open a book from the Home screen, tap Books to open the Books library. Locate the book you want to read (swipe upward if you need to reveal more books in the list) and simply tap it. If the book has not been downloaded to your Kindle Fire HD, it will download in a few seconds.

If you've read part of the book, it opens automatically to the last page you read. This last read page is bookmarked in the Cloud by Amazon when you stop reading, so no matter what device you use to read it — your Kindle Fire HD, computer, or smartphone, for example — you go to the last read page immediately.

Figure 6-3: The Grid view in the Books library.

You can also open a publication from Favorites or the Carousel. Read more about these features in Chapter 2.

Navigating a book

Your Kindle Fire HD provides you with several ways to move around your book.

The simplest way to move one page forward or one page back is to tap your finger anywhere on the right or left side of the page, respectively. With a book page displayed, tap the center of the page to see the tools along the bottom of the screen shown in Figure 6-5, including:

- ✓ A button in the bottom-left corner to take you to the Kindle Fire HD Home screen
- ✓ A Back button to go back one screen
- ✓ A Search button in the middle of the screen to initiate a search for text in the book.

Figure 6-4: New titles are easily identifiable.

In addition, along the top of the screen you find these options:

- ✔ A Settings menu to make adjustments to the appearance of fonts and the page
- ✔ A Go To button to access additional locations in the book
- ✔ A Notes button to display any notes you have made in the book
- ✔ An X-Ray button to display additional information about the book, if available for this title
- ✔ A Share button to share your thoughts about the book via Twitter or Facebook
- ✔ A Bookmark tool to place a bookmark on the page

The Progress bar along the bottom of the screen indicates how far along in the publication you are at the moment. To move around the publication, you can press the circle on this bar and drag it in either direction.

Options

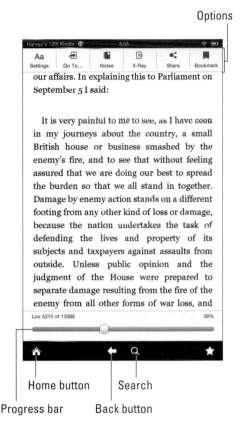

Home button   Search

Progress bar   Back button

Figure 6-5: Page of a book as displayed in the Kindle e-reader.

Searching in a book

Want to find that earlier reference to a character so that you can keep up with a plot? Or do you want to find any mention of Einstein in an e-encyclopedia? To find words or phrases in a book, you can use the Search feature.

Follow these steps to search a book:

1. **With a book open, tap the page to display the Option bar, if it's not already showing.**

Reading children's books

Some children's books with extensive illustrations use what Amazon refers to as a *fixed layout,* meaning that the pages are fixed representations of how the pages look in the print book. This means that you can't enlarge and reduce the size of everything on the page at one time, you can't change the font style, and you can't change orientation; each book is set in either landscape or portrait orientation. To move from page to page, you can swipe from right to left on the right page to flip it over.

Keep in mind that children's books are usually set up with blocks of text that go along with illustrations; that's why you can't enlarge text on an entire page; instead, you enlarge a single block of text. To do this, double-tap a block of text and the text becomes larger. When you subsequently swipe the page, you move to the next block of text, which enlarges (making the previous block of text go back to normal size).

At any time, you can double-tap the currently enlarged text again to go back to normal text size and proceed through the book.

Although the Option bar choices and Progress bar are the same as in other books, pressing the Font button in a children's book may result in the message `Font Style Options Are Not Available for This Title.`

2. **Tap the Search button at the bottom of the page.**

   The Search dialog box and onscreen keyboard are displayed.

3. **Enter a search term or phrase and then tap the Go key on the keyboard.**

   Search results are displayed, as shown in Figure 6-6.

You can also search the web for a word or phrase in your book. Press your finger on the word to highlight it and then, in the resulting dialog box, tap the More button. You can tap Search in Book, Search Wikipedia, or Search the Web. Tap the Back button when you want to return to the e-reader app.

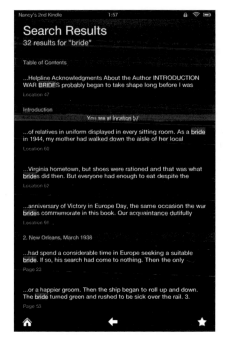

Figure 6-6: Search results indicate the search term with a highlight.

Bookmarking a page and highlighting text

If you find that perfect quote or a word you just have to read again at a later time, you can use the Bookmark feature.

To place a bookmark on a page, display the page and tap it in the center to reveal the Bookmark button (in the top-right corner of the page). Tap the Bookmark button. A small bookmark ribbon appears on the page.

To highlight text, press and hold your finger on the text and then drag your finger through the text. Small, triangular handles appear on either side of the text, as shown in Figure 6-7. If you want to select additional adjacent text to be highlighted, press your finger on one of these handles and drag to the left or right. When the entire phrase or paragraph that you want to highlight is selected, tap Highlight.

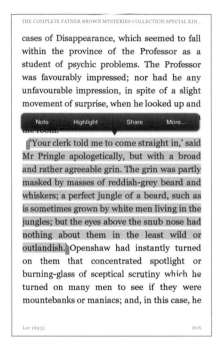

THE COMPLETE FATHER BROWN MYSTERIES COLLECTION SPECIAL KIN...

cases of Disappearance, which seemed to fall within the province of the Professor as a student of psychic problems. The Professor was favourably impressed; nor had he any unfavourable impression, in spite of a slight movement of surprise, when he looked up and the room.

| Note | Highlight | Share | More... |

'Your clerk told me to come straight in,' said Mr Pringle apologetically, but with a broad and rather agreeable grin. The grin was partly masked by masses of reddish-grey beard and whiskers; a perfect jungle of a beard, such as is sometimes grown by white men living in the jungles; but the eyes above the snub nose had nothing about them in the least wild or outlandish. Openshaw had instantly turned on them that concentrated spotlight or burning-glass of sceptical scrutiny which he turned on many men to see if they were mountebanks or maniacs; and, in this case, he

Loc 16935   86%

Figure 6-7: Press and drag either handle to enlarge the area of selected text.

You can display a list of bookmarks and highlights by tapping Notes (see Figure 6-8). You can jump to the page indicated by a bookmark, or jump to the highlighted text, by tapping an item in this list.

When you press and hold text, a brief definition appears from the pre-installed New American Oxford Dictionary. In the definition window, tap Full Definition to go to the full Oxford dictionary definition.

Modifying the appearance of a page

To control how elements appear on a page in the Kindle e-reader, tap the page to display the Options bar and then tap the Settings button (the one with a capital and lowercase *A: Aa*). The options, shown in Figure 6-9, appear as follows:

✔ **Font Size:** Tap the small or large font buttons to progressively decrease or increase the font size.

✔ **Color Mode (White, Sepia, Black):** Tap a setting to display a different color for the page's background. A sepia background may make reading easier on your eyes, for example.

✔ **Margins:** Choose the margin setting you prefer.

✔ **Font:** Select a different font for the page.

Note: Also available in Settings is the Text-to-Speech option, which is available for most books. Tap the On button to turn on Text-to-Speech. Then tap outside the Options window to view the current page of the book. Tap the center of the page to bring up the Progress bar and you see a Play button to the left of the Progress bar. Tap Play to listen to Text-to-Speech and your Kindle Fire HD will read the book to you! After it starts playing, you can adjust the speed of the reading by tapping the button to the right of the Progress bar — from a speedy 4 times normal speed to a slow 0.7 times normal speed.

Figure 6-8: Both highlights and bookmarks are listed.

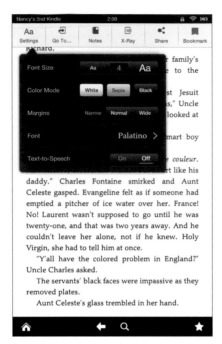

Figure 6-9: Font options offer you some control over the appearance of your pages.

Sharing with others

You can share with others your thoughts about books you've read via Facebook or Twitter. Follow these steps to share your thoughts on a book:

1. **With a book open in the Book library, tap the screen to view features at the top of the display.**

2. **Tap Share.**

3. **In the screen that appears, tap in the text field at the top of the page and use the onscreen keyboard to enter a message.**

Buying and Reading Periodicals

Reading magazines and newspapers on your Kindle Fire HD is similar to reading books on the device, but with a few important differences. You navigate magazines a bit differently and can display them in two different views.

Follow these steps to buy and read a magazine or newspaper:

1. **From the Home screen, tap Newsstand.**

2. **Tap Store.**

3. **Tap a periodical and then tap Subscribe Now or Buy Issue to buy it.**

4. **Return to Newsstand and tap a magazine or newspaper in the Newsstand to read it.**

   Alternatively, you can tap an item on the Carousel from the Home screen.

   If the publication hasn't been downloaded to the device, it begins to download now.

   With the Options bar visible (tap near the edge of the screen), thumbnails of all pages in the publication are displayed along the bottom of the screen (see Figure 6-10).

5. **Swipe right or left to scroll through these pages, or drag the scroll bar indicator left or right.**

6. **When you find the page you want, tap that page to display it full screen.**

   The Menu button on the Options bar displays contents of the current issue.

7. **Tap an item in the table of contents to go to that item.**

 As with books, in most publications you can double-tap to enlarge text on the page, and you double-tap again to reduce the size of the text. You can also pinch and unpinch your fingers on the touchscreen to move between larger and smaller views of a page's contents.

Figure 6-10: Scroll through thumbnails of pages to find the one you want.

Some periodicals can appear in two views:

- **Text view:** In Text view, you see articles in more of an e-reader format (meaning that you get larger text with no columns and no images). If a publication supports Text view, double-tapping the screen presents the contents in that view. In Text view, the Options bar has a Font button that offers Font Style and Typeface tabs to adjust the size and font used for text. Also available on the Options bar is a Style choice for changing Size, Margins, and Color Mode.

- **Page view:** Page view shows an exact image of the publication's pages, with all columns and photos intact. You can scroll through the magazine, view it in landscape or portrait orientation, and pinch and unpinch your fingers on the touchscreen to zoom in and out of the pages.

Double-tap to return from Text view to Page view.

In Page view, you can tap the Font tool on the Options bar to turn the page curl effect off. This effect seems to roll the current page as you flick with your finger to flip to the next page.

Reading Docs on Kindle Fire HD

Reading your personal documents ("docs") on your Kindle Fire HD is a much more basic activity than reading e-books. Docs give you fewer ways to navigate in them or format the appearance of text. To locate a document, tap the Docs button on the Home screen and tap its name. Or you can tap a doc on the Carousel or Favorites to open it.

Swipe left or right to move from page to page, or use the slider that displays along the bottom when the Options bar is active to move around the document.

You can read more about docs and the Kindle Fire HD in Chapter 10.

Chapter 7
Playing Music

*W*ith your Kindle Fire HD, you can listen to everything from Lady Gaga to Mozart, everywhere from the subway to the jogging path.

The ability to tap into Amazon's tremendous Music store (with more than 20 million songs) and transfer music from other sources means that you can build up your ideal music library and take it with you wherever you go. Also, Kindle Fire HD's Dolby Digital Plus stereo speakers, audio powered through dual drivers, provides one of the finest listening experiences in the world of tablets.

In this chapter, you learn about getting music onto your Kindle Fire HD and how to use the simple tools in the library to play your music and create playlists.

Exploring the Music Library

All your music is stored in the Music library (see Figure 7-1), which you display by tapping Music on the Kindle Fire HD Home screen. The currently playing or last played song and playback controls are located at the bottom of the screen.

Tap any of the Playlists, Artists, Albums, and Songs options to display the associated content.

Currently playing selection

Figure 7-1: The Music library is your central music repository.

Look to the bottom of the screen at the Options bar. There you find a Back arrow to move you back one screen in the library, the Menu icon, and a Search icon to help you find pieces of music.

If you tap the Menu button, you see additional options:

- ✔ **List View:** This displays your music with smaller icons in a list rather than a grid view.

- ✔ **Downloads:** Tap Downloads to see items in the process of downloading, as well as completed downloads.

- ✔ **Clear Player:** This setting appears in the menu only when you're displaying the currently playing music. If you are displaying the full screen of the currently playing music, tap the Clear Queue command to stop the music and go back to the Music library home screen.

- ✔ **Help:** Tap Help to get more information about using the Music app.

Music library settings

If you tap and drag down from the top of Kindle Fire HD's screen and then tap More in the Settings bar, you can then tap Applications, scroll down, and tap Music. When you do, you see two settings:

🖋 **Clear Cache.** This clears any data that has been stored to speed up future music downloads.

🖋 **Automatic Downloads.** This setting allows you to choose to automatically download selections to your Kindle Fire HD whenever you save them to the Amazon Cloud.

 When you tap the Search button on the Options bar, you bring up a search field. Tap in the field and enter the title of a piece of music or the name of a performer, and then tap Go on the onscreen keyboard. The Kindle Fire HD displays results for artists, albums, and songs in the Music library that match the search term(s).

Uploading Music to the Cloud

In addition to buying music from the Amazon Music store, you can transfer the music already stored on your computer. You can transfer it by using a micro-USB cable connection, as described in Chapter 2. Or you can use the process described in the upcoming steps to upload the music on your computer to the Amazon Cloud.

 Any MP3s you've purchased online from Amazon are stored in the Amazon Cloud. For items you've imported, the first 250 are stored for free.

After you've uploaded your music, it becomes available to you through your Kindle Fire HD Music library.

Follow these steps to upload music to the Amazon Cloud:

    1. **Go to** www.amazon.com/cloudplayer **on your PC or Mac.**

2. **Sign into your Amazon account.**

3. **Click the Import Your Music button.**

   A dialog box appears, asking you to get the Amazon Music Importer.

4. **Click Download Now and follow the instructions that appear to install the Importer.**

   After the Importer has been installed, click to authorize your device, and you see the Amazon Cloud Player dialog box shown in Figure 7-2.

5. **Click the Start Scan button.**

   If you'd rather pick the items to import yourself, click the Browse Manually button at this point. The following screen lists the number of songs that our scan found.

6. **Click the Import Now button.**

The dialog box shows your import progress.

Figure 7-2: Tap into all your music by using the Importer.

After you upload items to your Amazon Cloud library, they are available to the Kindle Fire HD on the Cloud side of the Music library (see Figure 7-3).

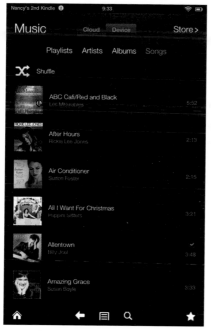

Figure 7-3: Music you've stored in the Amazon Cloud Player is listed in your Kindle Fire HD library.

Playing Music

After you have some music available to play, playing that music is an easy task.

Opening and playing a song

Follow these steps to play music from your Music library:

1. **Tap Music on the Kindle Fire HD Home screen.**

2. **Locate an item that you want to play by using an option in the Music library, such as Songs or Artists.**

3. **If you open an option other than Songs, you need to tap to open an album or playlist to view the contents.**

4. **Tap to play the song.**

   If you tap the first song in a group of music selections, such as an album or playlist, the Kindle Fire HD begins to play all selections, starting with the one you tapped.

5. **Use the controls shown in Figure 7-4 to control playback.**

Figure 7-4: Most of these tools are standard playback tools that you've probably seen before.

Tap the back-facing arrow on the Options bar or the Hide
button in the top-left corner of a currently playing song to
go back to the album or playlist that the song belongs to.
To go back to the Now Playing screen for the song, tap the information bar for the song that appears along the bottom of the
screen (see Figure 7-5).

Figure 7-5: The currently playing song sports a little orange speaker in
this list.

You can adjust playback volume by using the Volume setting in
the Now Playing controls or you can use the physical volume
buttons.

Getting sound out by cord or Bluetooth

If you want to use a headphone with your Kindle Fire HD, which can improve the sound and remove extraneous noise, plug a compatible headphone into the headphone jack at the side of the device, near the Power button.

Alternatively, you can use the Kindle Fire HD's Bluetooth capability to connect to a Bluetooth headset or speakers. To enable Bluetooth in the Settings, tap Wireless and then tap Bluetooth. Tap the Enable Bluetooth On button. Kindle Fire HD searches for nearby Bluetooth devices, but if it doesn't find yours, you can manually initiate a scan by tapping the Search for Devices button.

Creating playlists

Playlists allow you to create collections of songs that transcend the boundaries of albums or artists. For example, you might want to create a playlist for a romantic evening, a dance party, or a road trip.

When you tap Music on the Home screen, you see the Playlists option (see Figure 7-6). Tap it and you see a Create New Playlist button and two default playlists, Purchases and Recently Added to Cloud. If you have created other playlists, they appear on this screen as well.

To create a new playlist, follow these steps:

1. **Connect to a Wi-Fi network if you aren't already connected.**

   Creating a playlist requires a Wi-Fi connection because playlists are saved to the Cloud.

2. **Tap Playlists from the top of the Music library screen. Then tap the Create New Playlist box.**

3. **In the screen that appears, enter a playlist name and tap Save.**

   The Kindle Fire HD displays a screen containing a Search field and a list of songs stored on the device.

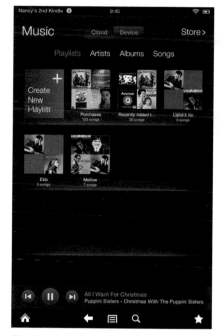

Figure 7-6: You can store the items that you buy and download in playlists.

4. **Tap the Add Song (+) button to the right of any song to select it.**

   If you want to find a song without scrolling down the list, enter a song name in the Search field until the list narrows down to display it.

5. **Tap Done to save your playlist.**

   The Playlist is displayed (see Figure 7-7).

You can play the newly created playlist by simply tapping Playlist, tapping the list you want to play, and then tapping the song you want to play.

When you tap the Edit button on a playlist, you see an Add Songs button and a Done button in the Edit screen. Songs appear with a Delete (–) symbol next to them; tap this symbol to delete a song. Tap the Add Songs button to choose more songs to add to the playlist. Finally, tap Done when you're done editing.

Edit button

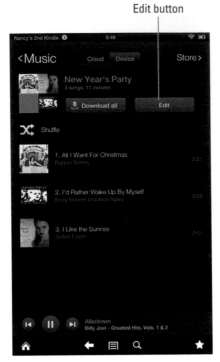

Figure 7-7: A saved playlist.

Chapter 8

Playing Video

. . . .

In This Chapter

▶ Streaming or downloading videos

▶ Poring over your Video library

▶ Watching movies and TV shows

▶ Using X-Ray for Movies

. . . .

*P*laying video is a great use of the Kindle Fire HD. The device has a bright, crisp screen, can easily be held in one hand, and is capable of streaming video from the Amazon Cloud. Amazon offers an amazing selection of video content.

You can discover the ins and outs of buying video content in Chapter 4. In this chapter, we explain how Amazon streams video content from the Cloud to your device, give you a look at the Kindle Fire HD Video library, and cover the steps involved in playing a video.

Streaming versus Downloading

When you tap Video on the Kindle Fire HD Home screen, you're immediately taken to the Amazon Video Store (see Figure 8-1) rather than to a library of video titles. That makes sense because, by design, Kindle Fire HD is best used to stream videos from the Cloud rather than play them from a library on the device. To go to your Video library, all you have to do is tap Library in the top-right corner.

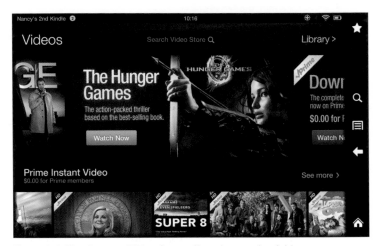

Figure 8-1: The Amazon Video Store offers thousands of titles.

Video content in the Video Store might include Prime Instant Videos, a feature that offers thousands of titles for free with an Amazon Prime account. (You get one free month of Amazon Prime with your Kindle Fire HD, after which you can purchase a membership for $79 a year.) You can also purchase or rent other video programs and stream them from the Cloud.

Amazon's Whispersync technology keeps track of the spot in a video where you stopped watching on any device. You can later resume watching that video at that exact location on Kindle Fire HD, a PC or Mac, or one of more than 300 compatible TVs, Blu-ray Disc players, or other devices.

You *can* download videos that you purchase, which is useful if you want to watch them away from a Wi-Fi connection. (You can't download Prime Instant Videos, however.) It's a good idea to remove a video from the device when you're done with it to save space, and you can get it again whenever you want from the Cloud, where it remains stored. To delete a video from your device, open the Video library and tap Device. Press and hold your finger on the video; then tap Remove from Device in the menu that appears.

Looking at Your Video Library

We're betting that you'll find viewing video on your Kindle Fire HD to be a great way to get your entertainment. The Kindle Fire HD Video library may become your favorite destination for buying, viewing, and organizing your video content.

When you tap Video on your Kindle Fire HD Home screen, the Amazon Video store opens (refer to Figure 8-1).

The Video store shows three video categories: Featured Videos, Prime Instant Videos, and Your Watchlist.

 Watchlist is a way to make note of items that you may want to watch in the future; you can add any video to your Watchlist by tapping and holding it and then tapping Add to Watchlist in the menu that appears.

Tap any video in the Featured list or Watchlist to get more details about it, or tap the category title Prime Instant Video to see more items in that category.

 When you tap the All button in the Video store, you see all items organized by popularity.

Tap Library to go to your Video library (see Figure 8-2). The library sports two options: one lists all your videos stored in the Cloud; the other includes videos you've purchased that have been downloaded to the device. The option that has orange lettering is the active one.

You can also see two options for filtering videos by Movies or TV programs. Tap the Search button in the Options bar to search for a particular video.

 Downloaded video content is listed chronologically by the date you downloaded it.

Figure 8-2: The Kindle Fire HD Video library stored in the Amazon Cloud.

Tap the Menu button on the Options bar to display two items: Settings and Help. In Settings, you can view the Device ID and access the Disable HD Purchase Warning setting. If you disable this feature, it turns off a warning that tells you that although you can play high-definition videos on the Kindle Fire HD, they won't play in high definition because it's not a high-definition device.

 You can tap the Menu button in the Options bar and then tap Your Watchlist to view the videos you've set aside in a list for future viewing.

Opening and Playing a Video

Playing a video is a simple process. If the video has been downloaded to your device, open the library (tap Videos and then tap Library), locate the video, and then tap the video to play it. If you've played the video before, you may have to tap a Resume, Start Over, or Download button to get it going again (see Figure 8-3).

Figure 8-3: Start again or resume where you left off.

If a video that you want to stream for the first time is stored in the Cloud, follow these steps:

1. **Tap Cloud from the Videos screen.**

   Videos you've rented (whose rental period hasn't expired) or purchased are displayed.

2. **Tap an item to open it.**

   If it's a TV show, you see episodes listed (see Figure 8-4). Tap one to open it or tap the Buy button to buy an entire season. If it's a movie, at this point you see a description of the movie and the option of watching it or downloading it (see Figure 8-5).

3. **Tap the Watch Now button.**

   The playback controls appear.

4. **If you've already watched part of the video, tap the Resume button (refer to Figure 8-3).**

   If you'd rather watch from its start a video that you've seen previously, tap the Play from Beginning button.

Figure 8-4: The episode list for a grim TV show.

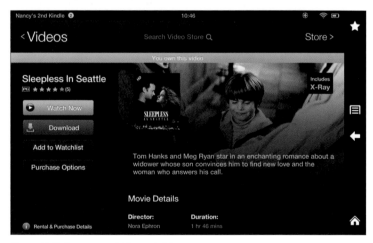

Figure 8-5: A new movie to watch!

The Kindle Fire HD screen provides an extra-wide viewing angle. This means that you and those watching with you can see the content from the side as well as from straight on.

The familiar playback tools available here include:

- Play
- Pause
- A progress bar
- A volume slider
- A 10s button that moves you ten seconds back in the video
- In the case of TV shows, a Next Episode button

You can also find a Back button in the Options bar that you can tap to stop playback and return to the Kindle Fire HD Video library.

 When you display a video's details in the Amazon Video store, you can tap the Rental & Purchase Details link to view the terms of use for playing the video.

Using X-Ray for Movies

The X-Ray feature works with some books and movies to give you access to facts about what you're reading or watching.

In the case of movies, this feature provides information about the cast (see Figure 8-6), and if you tap a particular cast member, you get details about that person's career and other movies he or she has appeared in (Figure 8-7).

To display X-Ray information, all you have to do is tap the screen when a movie is playing and the cast list appears in the upper-left corner. Tap See Full Cast List to see the entire list and then tap one to see details like those shown in Figure 8-7.

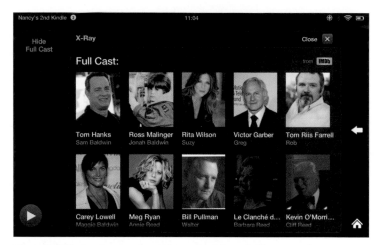

Figure 8-6: Find out more about the cast while watching a movie.

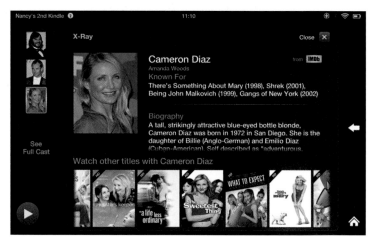

Figure 8-7: If you like a star of a movie, look for other movies featuring her here.

Chapter 9
Going Social

*K*indle Fire isn't just about watching movies and playing music. You have several ways to use the device to interact and communicate with others.

In this chapter, we help you explore how Kindle Fire helps you keep in touch with people using the pre-installed Contacts app. We explore how Kindle Fire integrates with Facebook and tell you all about using the Skype app. You also find out about the new Kindle Fire HD camera and microphone that you use to make calls over the Internet with Skype.

Managing Contacts

The Contacts app pre-installed on the Kindle Fire is a basic but useful contact management tool. You can enter or import contact information, sort that information by several criteria, and use Contacts to address e-mails.

You can find Contacts by tapping Apps on the Kindle Fire Home screen. Tap the Contacts app to display its main screen, as shown in Figure 9-1.

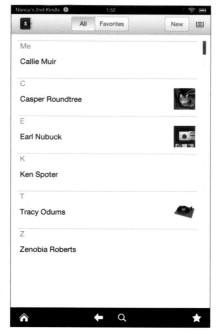

Figure 9-1: The Contacts app main screen with several contacts entered.

Importing contacts

If you have associated an e-mail account with your Kindle Fire HD, you can import all contacts from that account rather than enter each contact individually. (See Chapter 5 for setting up e-mail to sync with your Kindle Fire HD.)

After you have set up an associated e-mail account, open Contacts and tap the New button. Tap the account from which you want to import contacts when you see the message shown in Figure 9-2. Your contacts are imported.

Figure 9-2: Synchronize to import contacts from your e-mail account.

Creating new contacts

It's data entry time! Importing contacts (see preceding section) is a nice shortcut, but you can also manually enter contacts by adding their information in the New Contact form.

To create a new contact, follow these steps:

1. **Tap the E-mail app in the Apps library. Tap the Menu icon at the bottom of the screen and then tap Contacts. Tap the Menu icon again and select the option for adding a new contact.**

   The New Contact screen that appears (see Figure 9-3) contains fields including First Name, Last Name, Phone, and so on.

Figure 9-3: The New Contact screen.

2. **Tap in a field and enter text.**

   The onscreen keyboard appears when you tap in a field.

3. **When you've entered text in one field, tap the Next button on the keyboard to go to the next field.**

   Be sure to scroll to the bottom and enter detailed address information. You tap Add Another Field at the bottom of the form to choose additional information fields to include.

4. **Tap the Photo icon at the top of the form and then tap Add Photo to add a photo.**

   Options appear for selecting photos.

5. **Tap a photo source such as Photos to open it, double-tap to open a photo album, and then tap a photo to add it to the contact record.**

6. **Tap Save.**

The contact information displays as shown.

To edit the contact, tap the Edit button. To display all contacts, tap the All button.

Viewing contacts

You can use settings to control how your contacts are organized and even save contacts to a list of Favorites in the Contacts app.

To sort your contacts, follow these steps:

1. **On the bar across the top of the Contacts list, tap the Menu button and then tap Settings.**

   The E-mail, Contacts, and Calendar settings appear.

2. **Tap Contacts General Settings.**

3. **Tap Sort Order of Contact Name to display the options shown in Figure 9-4.**

4. **Tap to sort by first name or last name.**

   Tap each setting and choose your sort preference from the list that appears.

You can also choose to view contacts in the Favorites area of the Home screen. To add a contact to Favorites, follow these steps:

1. **Tap Apps and then tap Contacts to open the Contacts app.**

2. **Tap the All tab.**

3. **Tap the contact name you want to make a favorite.**

4. **Tap the star that appears next to the contact's name.**

   The star turns blue, indicating that this is a favorite.

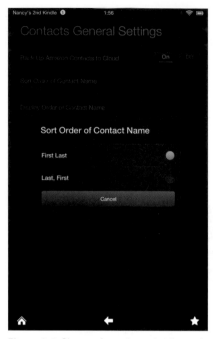

Figure 9-4: Choose from these basic sorting options.

Using Integrated Facebook, Twitter, and Amazon Social Features

If you want to work with your Facebook and Twitter accounts from your Kindle Fire HD, you can download those free apps from the Appstore. Even easier, though, you can share items through Amazon or via Facebook and Twitter using tools integrated into your Kindle Fire HD itself.

For example, when you are reading a book, tap the screen to display tools. Tap the Share button at the top of the screen. Doing so offers you the options shown in Figure 9-5. Simply enter a comment. If you want to share via Facebook or Twitter, just tap one of those options and a screen like the one shown in Figure 9-6 appears. Tap Connect and, if necessary, sign into your account to post your comment to Facebook or Twitter.

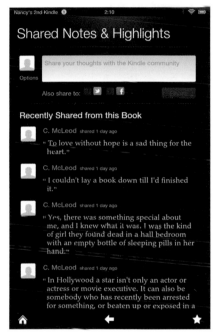

Figure 9-5: Share comments with others on Amazon.

You can also compare your game progress with Facebook friends when you join GameCircle. When you tap the Games library on the Home screen, you see the screen shown in Figure 9-7. Tap the Connect button and you can create a connection between your Amazon account and Facebook. You can then share your scores and achievements on Facebook and add any Facebook friends who have joined GameCircle.

Figure 9-6: Share via your Facebook or Twitter account.

Figure 9-7: Turn on Facebook for GameCircle here.

Making Calls with Skype

The Kindle Fire HD comes with a camera and microphone. Although you can't (currently) take photos or videos, you can make video calls to others using Skype. The Skype app for Kindle Fire HD is free, but you will have to download it from the Appstore. (See Chapter 4 for more about getting apps.)

When you have downloaded the app, you tap Apps from the Home Screen and then tap the Skype app to open it. On the Welcome to Skype screen, tap Continue, tap Accept on the following screen to accept terms and conditions, and then follow these steps to begin using the app:

1. **In the screen shown in Figure 9-8, enter a Skype Name and Password.**

Figure 9-8: If you have a Skype account, enter your information here.

If you've never created a Skype account, tap the Create an Account button at this point and enter your name, Skype Name, a password, e-mail address, and phone number to create your Skype account.

2. **Tap the Sign In button and, on the next screen, tap Continue.**

   On the screen that appears, you can tap three options to make calls:

   - **Tap Contacts:** This displays a list of contacts saved in your Kindle Fire Contacts app. Tap one and then tap the Call button (it's green and shows a little phone handset in it, as shown in Figure 9-9) to place a call.

   - **Tap Recent:** This displays recently made calls so that you can tap one to call the person again.

   - **Tap Call Phones:** This displays a screen where you can enter the number you want to call in the field at the top of the screen. Then tap the Call button to place the call.

Here are a few more tips to remember about using Skype on your Kindle Fire HD:

✓ You need to have credits to call people who aren't Skype users. Go to www.skype.com and sign in with your account information to buy credits.

✓ From the Skype main screen on Kindle Fire HD, you can tap the Profile button and enter a message that's shared with all your contacts, such as the phone number you use to accept Skype calls.

✓ You can tap the Settings button in the top-right corner of the Skype app main screen to access settings for receiving incoming calls, syncing contacts, signing in automatically, and so on, as shown in Figure 9-10.

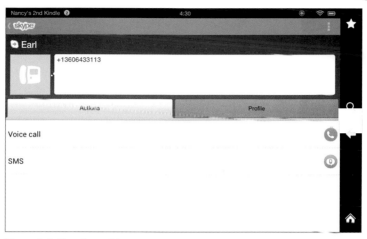

Figure 9-9: Tap the call button to place a call.

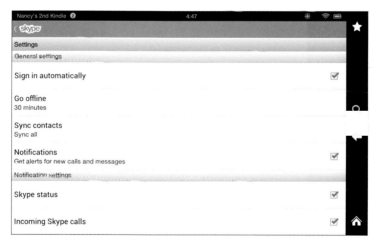

Figure 9-10: You can control your incoming and outgoing call experience with these settings.

Chapter 10

Getting Productive with Kindle Fire HD

*K*indle Fire HD isn't just about watching movies and playing music. You have several ways to use the device to get your work done and share documents and images with others.

In this chapter, we help you explore how Kindle Fire HD helps you view and share documents. The new, pre-installed Calendar app, which we cover in this chapter, is useful for keeping on schedule. Also, the Photos app lets you view or edit photos for work or play, as explained in this chapter.

Understanding Kindle Docs

One of the items you see across the top of your Kindle Fire HD Home screen is the Docs library. This is where you can view your personal documents (see Figure 10-1). You can also save docs to Favorites on the Home screen, or upload docs from your computer to the Amazon Cloud.

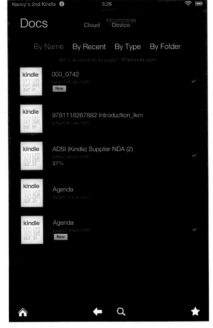

Figure 10-1: Tap Docs from the Home screen to open the Docs library.

In the following sections, you see how docs get onto your Kindle Fire HD and how you can view and share them. We also provide some advice about using productivity software on Kindle Fire HD to get your work done.

Getting docs onto the Kindle Fire HD

To get a doc onto your Kindle Fire HD, you can transfer it from your PC or Mac by using the included micro-USB connector, or you can send it to your device at your Kindle e-mail address. (Locate this address by opening your Docs library; it's listed under the sort options near the top of the screen.)

Documents come in different formats. Kindle Fire HD supports a variety of document formats, including TXT, Microsoft Word DOCX, HTML, RTF, and PDF, as well as Amazon's MOBI or ASW formats.

If you send a document to your Kindle e-mail address, the file appears in your Docs library automatically. Kindle formats (MOBI and AZW) are also supported, and some documents will be converted to this format automatically. Kindle Fire HD even supports compressed (ZIP) file formats and automatically unzips them when they're transferred to your device via e-mail.

Although you can view these documents, as shown in Figure 10-2, you can't edit them on your Kindle Fire HD without downloading an app such as OfficeSuite Pro.

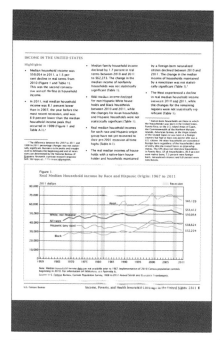

Figure 10-2: A PDF document displayed on the Kindle Fire HD.

To transfer docs to your Kindle Fire HD, grab the micro-USB cable that came with Kindle Fire HD and follow these steps:

1. **Attach the micro-USB end of the cable to your Kindle Fire HD.**

2. **Attach the USB end of the cable to your computer.**

    Your Kindle Fire HD appears as a drive labeled "Kindle" in Windows Explorer (Windows) or Finder (Mac).

3. **Click the Kindle drive to open and view files on the drive (see Figure 10-3).**

4. **Double-click the Internal Storage folder and then click and drag files from your hard drive to the Docs folder in the Kindle Fire HD window.**

   Drag documents to the Documents folder, pictures to the Photos folder, audio files to the Music folder, and so on.

5. **Tap the Disconnect button on your Kindle Fire HD to safely eject the Kindle Fire HD from your computer.**

You can now unplug the micro-USB cord from your Kindle Fire HD and computer.

 After you've sent personal documents to your device using your Send-to-Kindle e-mail address, your documents are automatically stored in the Amazon Cloud, where you can download them to any other Kindle device you may have.

Figure 10-3: Your Kindle Fire HD appears like an external drive on your computer when attached using a micro-USB cable.

Opening docs

After you put a doc onto your Kindle Fire HD by either transferring it from a computer or receiving it through Kindle e-mail, you can view the document by following these steps:

1. **Tap Docs on the Kindle Fire HD Home screen to open the Docs library.**

2. **When the library opens (see Figure 10-4), tap a sort option, if desired, to change the order of the displayed documents.**

   You can sort by these options: By Name, By Recent, or By Type. If you are looking at docs in your Cloud account, you can also choose By Folder; you can create folders from the Amazon Cloud site.

3. **When you find the document you want to view, tap the arrow to the right of it to open it.**

At this point, all you can do is view a document, not edit it — although with documents using Microsoft Word format, you can add notes and highlights. However, you can't edit a document at all without a third-party app.

 To search for a document, tap the Search button in the Options bar, type a document name in the Search field, tap an option to search from among Libraries, Stores, or Web, and tap Go on the onscreen keyboard.

E-mailing docs

When you have a doc on your Kindle Fire HD, you can view it and also share it with others as an e-mail attachment. Follow these steps to attach a doc to an e-mail message:

Figure 10-4: The Docs library with sort options.

1. **Tap the Favorites button on the Home screen and tap the E-mail app.**

   The E-mail app opens.

2. **Tap your Inbox and then tap the New button.**

   A blank e-mail form appears.

3. **Enter a name in the To field, a subject, and a message.**

4. **Tap Options and then tap the Attach button.**

   In the menu that appears (see Figure 10-5), choose to attach an item from OfficeSuite or from your personal Photos or Videos. If you choose OfficeSuite you can then tap the My Documents folder to access all the documents in your Docs app. You can also choose Internal Storage, which will include folders for various libraries, including Music, Books, and Docs.

5. **Tap Send.**

Your document goes on its way, attached to your e-mail.

Figure 10-5: Attaching a doc to an e-mail message.

Taking documents further

If you want to edit documents on your Kindle Fire HD, consider OfficeSuite Pro (see Figure 10-6). This app will cost you $14.99, but it lets you both view and edit Microsoft Word and Excel documents as well as view Microsoft PowerPoint files.

If you open the OfficeSuite app that comes with your Kindle Fire HD, you can tap the Upgrade to OfficeSuite Pro icon in the lower-left corner to get the more robust app.

Figure 10-6: OfficeSuite Pro offers common office productivity tools.

Staying on Time with Calendar

The pre-installed Calendar app is new with Kindle Fire HD. The simple calendar interface allows you to sync with calendars from your e-mail account, view and edit events, and create new events.

Calendar views

Before you can use many of Calendar's features, you have to sync it with a calendar account, typically through your e-mail provider. When you first open Calendar, you see the blank calendar shown in Figure 10-7.

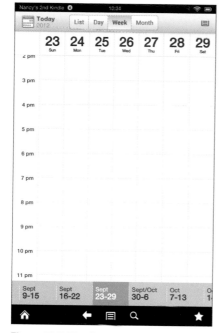

Figure 10-7: The Calendar app is a welcome addition to the Kindle Fire HD.

Tap a tab to display the calendar by Day, Week, or Month, or to display a List of events. Note that if you tap a date in the Month view, that date opens in Day view.

To move to other dates, use the buttons along the bottom of the screen. In Day view, these will be dates just before and after the currently displayed day; the buttons work similarly for Week and Month views.

Syncing with a calendar account

You can't add a new event until you sync with a calendar in an online account. To do so, tap the Menu button in the top-right corner, tap the New Event button, and follow these steps:

1. **Tap the Add Account button.**

2. **Tap an account in the list, such as AOL, Exchange, or Hotmail, or tap Other Provider for any other type of account.**

3. **On the screen shown in Figure 10-8, enter your account information and tap Next.**

   You may see a message about how POP access is required to get Plus features, if they're available for your account. Tap OK to proceed.

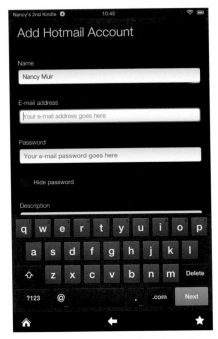

Figure 10-8: Enter information about the account you want to sync with Calendar.

Kindle Fire HD may take a few seconds to sync with your account. You return to Calendar and can now add and edit events. (Note that Amazon advises that you can't sync with AOL calendars.)

Creating a new Calendar event

Events are brought over from the calendar you sync with, but you can also add new events. With either Day or Week view displayed, follow these steps to add an event:

1. **Tap a date or time in the calendar. Tap the Menu icon in the top-right corner of the screen and then tap the New Event option.**

2. **The New Event form, shown in Figure 10-9, appears.**

Figure 10-9: Fill out this screen to add a new event to your calendar.

3. **Tap the words New Event and enter a title for the event.**

4. **Tap in the From time and date fields to choose a start time; do likewise with the To time and date fields.**

   If the event runs all day, skip the From and To field settings and simply tap the All Day check box.

5. **Tap the Repeat field if you want an event to repeat at a regular interval.**

6. **You can tap the Reminders field to choose to get an alert on your Kindle Fire HD at a certain interval before the event commences.**

7. **If you want to invite a person you've saved as a contact, tap the + (plus sign) button in the Invite field.**

8. **If you want, you can make entries in the Where and Notes fields.**

9. **Tap Save.**

   The event appears in your calendar.

To edit an event, simply tap to open it and then tap the Edit button.

Viewing Photos

Kindle Fire HD has a pre-installed Photos app for photography lovers, although its features are pretty basic. Still, Photos allows you to view your photos on the device's bright screen.

Getting photos onto Kindle Fire HD

You can take photos with the Kindle Fire camera. Tap Photos on the Home screen and then tap the Camera icon in the top-right corner. Aim your Kindle Fire at your subject and then tap the Capture button along the left side of the screen. The photo is saved, and you can open it in the Photos app by clicking on the thumbnail of it that appears in the lower-left corner. You can also save an image from the Internet by using your Silk browser or copy it from your computer by using your Micro USB cable. Using this procedure, you can copy photos into the Pictures folder on your Kindle Fire HD by using File Explorer or the Mac Finder.

Viewing photos

After you load photos into your Pictures library and disconnect the micro-USB cable, you can tap the Photos app on the Home screen. Doing so displays an album that represents the folder you copied to your Kindle Fire HD (see Figure 10-10) and other albums that you may have created from downloads of photos (from e-mail or the web) and screenshots. If you copy another folder of photos, it will come over as a separate album. Photos in albums are organized chronologically by the date you placed them on your Kindle Fire HD.

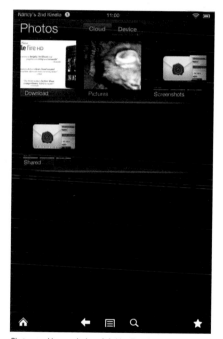

Photos used by permission of Ashley Ernstberger Photography

Figure 10-10: Photo albums in the Gallery.

You have the choice of three main actions to take to view pictures:

- ✔ Tap an album to open it and view the pictures within it.
- ✔ Tap a picture to make it appear full screen.
- ✔ Swipe left or right to move through pictures in an album.

You can also tap the E-mail button in the Options bar while in Photos to e-mail the displayed photo. Another method of sharing via e-mail is to tap the Options bar, tap Share, and then tap Send with Email. In the e-mail message that appears with the photo already attached, enter an address, subject, and message and then tap the Send button.

Managing photos in Cloud Drive

Another way to get your photos onto your Kindle Fire HD is to upload photos from your computer to Amazon's Cloud Drive. Cloud Drive provides up to 5GB of free storage of photos and easily transfers those photos to your Kindle Fire HD.

You have to install a free desktop app on your computer to use Cloud Drive. To do so, go to Amazon.com, tap Your Account, and then tap or click Your Cloud Drive on the list that appears. Then follow the onscreen instructions to install.

You can manage your Cloud Drive photos in two ways: Move photos from one album to another, and rename photos or photo albums:

- ✔ **Moving photos:** To move a photo, you need to go to the Amazon Cloud Drive using a browser (go to Amazon.com, tap Your Account, and then tap or click Your Cloud Drive on the list that appears). Use the More Actions drop-down list and choose Move X Items to (where X is the number of items you've selected) and then choose the folder on your Cloud Drive to move the item(s) to.

- ✔ **Rename:** You can rename a picture or albums from within Cloud Drive by tapping or clicking the More Actions button and then choosing Rename. You can also rename an album from your Kindle Fire HD by long-pressing the album (press and hold for a few seconds) and choosing Rename from the menu that appears.

Keeping your finger on the Pulse

Another neat app you can use to enlighten yourself is Pulse News, a free news aggregator. This app allows you to choose from among various sources of content, such as *The New Yorker* or ESPN Headlines, and then access them from one central location. You can download the Pulse News app from the App Store.

✔ **Rotate Left:** Tap this tool to rotate the image 180 degrees to the left.

✔ **Rotate Right:** Tap this tool to rotate the image 180 degrees to the right.

Note that you can also enlarge or reduce a photo by pinching and unpinching with your fingers on the touchscreen.

To delete a photo, simply tap the Trash button on the Options bar.

You can't retrieve an item after you've deleted it from your device, so do so with care! (If you transferred the item from your computer or from Cloud Drive, you can always retransfer it, of course.)

Chapter 11

Ten Apps That Add Functionality to Kindle Fire HD

*A*ny mobile device today, from a smartphone to a tablet, thrives on the thousands of apps that make a world of features available.

Kindle Fire HD has functionality built in for consuming books, periodicals, music, and video, as well as a contact management, calculator, and calendar app, web browser, and e-mail client. However, there are some tools that many of us have grown used to having available that you can easily acquire by adding apps to the device.

The Amazon Appstore, which you can learn more about in Chapter 4, contains thousands of cool apps for you to explore. To help you flesh out the basic tools in Kindle Fire HD, in this chapter we provide reviews of apps such as a note taker, alarm app, and unit converter that meet your day-to-day needs and whet your *app*etite. Most of these are free.

From a nutrition guide to a very cool drawing app, these will provide you with fun and useful functionality for your Kindle Fire HD and not cost you much more than the time to download them.

SketchBook Mobile

From: AutoDesk, Inc.

Price: $1.99

SketchBook (see Figure 11-1) is a drawing app to satisfy the creative artist in your soul. With 47 preset brushes, you can draw whatever you can imagine on your Kindle Fire HD screen. You can control the brush characteristics and make use of an extensive color palette.

Try transferring photos and modifying them with this clever app; then save your files in JPEG, PNG, or PSD formats. When you're done, it's easy to e-mail your artistic efforts to yourself to print from your computer.

The Brush Properties circular control lets you easily adjust the size and opacity of the writing tools. Touch the square at the top of the screen to access color controls and watch the Red, Blue, and Green levels adjust as you move around the color wheel.

However, be careful of the Erase button in the upper-left corner of the screen: We've erased more than one picture by tapping this when we shouldn't have!

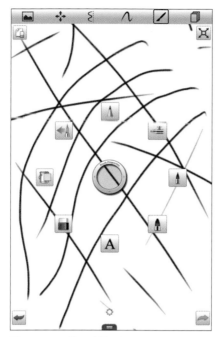

Figuro 11-1: SketchRnok brings out the artist in you.

Fast Food Nutrition Lite

From: FastFood.com

Price: Frcc

If you're watching your weight but are forced to scarf down fast food now and then, this little app could have an impact on your waistline. Not limited to traditional drive-thru fast food joints, the app gives you nutritional information about dishes from 100 restaurant chains, such as Applebee's, Chili's, and Checker's, and includes more than 25,000 menu items (see Figure 11-2).

Fast Food Nutrition Lite helps you keep track of calories, Weight Watchers points, fats, trans fats, saturated fats, cholesterol, sodium, carbohydrates, sugars, and protein. The calorie counter shows you how much of the recommended daily allowance each meal is providing you. Select the items you want in your meal and touch View Order, which displays a handy screen showing you all the totals for your meal.

	Search	Qty 0	Serving	Calories	Fat (g)	Sat Fat (g)	TransFat (g)	Cholest (mg)
Appetizers - as served								
Cheeseburger Sliders	0	1	1240	80	25	3	n/a	
Cheeseburger Sliders with Applewood Smoked Bacon	0	1	1310	85	27	3	n/a	
Chicken Quesadilla Grande	0	1	1440	87	37	2	n/a	
Cheese Quesadilla Grande	0	1	1270	84	36	2	n/a	
Pork Wonton Tacos	0	1	940	47	14	0	n/a	
Chicken Wonton Tacos	0	1	610	24	5	0	n/a	
Mozzarella Sticks	0	1	940	46	20	1	n/a	
Crunchy Onion Rings	0	1	1230	59	11	1	n/a	
Appetizer Sampler	0	1	2510	168	49	3	n/a	
Spinach & Artichoke Dip	0	1	1600	107	30	1	n/a	
Boneless Buffalo Wings, Classic	0	1	1170	69	16	1	n/a	
Boneless Buffalo Wings, Hot	0	1	1170	70	16	1	n/a	
Boneless Buffalo Wings, Honey BBQ	0	1	1240	55	11	1	n/a	
Boneless Buffalo Wings,	0	1	1110	55	11	1	n/a	

Figure 11-2: Keep track of your calories with this handy counter.

You can add thumbnails for your favorite restaurants so that you don't have to search through all the restaurants to find the ones you like best.

You sometimes pay a different kind of price to get an app that costs no money. In the case of this app, and several others, that price is having to view ads as you use the app.

Alarm Clock Xtreme Free

From: Angle Labs, Inc.

Price: Free

Kindle Fire HD has no built-in alarm app, so this one is a natural to add to your apps collection. This easy-to-use alarm app can help keep you on schedule (see Figure 11-3). You can create and edit alarms and control how far ahead of events and at what intervals you're alerted to alarms.

Figure 11-3: Get alarms to get you going on time.

You can set a timer with this app and have the app display a countdown to the event. (Count down to Christmas; count down to your wedding day? Your choice!) You can change the look and feel of the alarm app with different colored backgrounds and a large snooze button.

Astral Budget

From: Astral Web, Inc.

Price: Free

If you're like many of us these days, you're tightening your belt and counting those pennies. Astral Budget is an app that helps you keep track of all your expenses, whether for a single trip or your yearly household budget. You can use built-in categories for fixed spending such as rent, food, travel, utilities, and so on to categorize your expenses.

The app has four sections: Goals, Expense, Reports, and Export (see Figure 11-4). Using these, you can enter the amounts you want to spend and track them against actual expenditures. You can use the wide variety of Reports in Astral Budget to examine your spending trends and even export data to your computer to examine with the more robust application Excel. We like the Chart selections, including bar charts, pie charts, and list charts.

Figure 11-4: Use various tools to enter and visualize your spending practices.

ColorNote Notepad Notes

From: Social & Mobile, Inc.

Price: Free

Kindle Fire HD doesn't include a note-taking app, and if you're like us, you need one. If being able to keep a to-do list warms the cockles of your organized (or disorganized) heart, this is a neat little free app and is very simple to use.

You can keep a simple to-do list or other random notes and even share information with your friends via e-mail, social networks, or messaging (honey, here's the shopping list for your evening commute!).

ColorNote allows some nice word-processing-like functions, such as the ability to edit and delete items off lists that are completed (see Figure 11-5).

Figure 11-5: When you finish an item on your list, delete it.

You can even set up reminders for items in your notes and search for specific content.

If your notes are top secret, consider using the password feature in ColorNote.

Cube Calculator

From: IP

Price: Free

It's a good idea to add a calculator to Kindle Fire HD, if only to figure out tips and your sales commissions, right? This is a calculator with tons of bells and whistles, from the ability to use mathematical expressions and time calculations to logarithmic and trigonometric functions. This app provides a secondary keyboard for additional functions, such as cosines (see Figure 11-6).

Figure 11-6: The keyboard sports bold fonts and is easy to use.

Even if you're not a power math user, the very nice interface in this app makes casual calculations simple to do. Also, the help system for this app is actually helpful.

You can choose a theme such as Light or Dark to ease your eyestrain as you calculate. You can also control the maximum number of digits to be returned in a result (after all, who needs pi to go on ad infinitum?).

Handrite Note Pro

From: Ben Lee

Price: $2.99

If you miss the feeling of writing notes by hand rather than typing them on keyboards, this app is for you. It's simple to use: Tap to create a new note and then use the spiral-bound pad interface to write words or draw images on the page with your finger. You can change the stroke width and text size for your writing and even use different colors (see Figure 11-7).

When you close the app, your note is saved, but you can press and hold the touchscreen to edit the text you entered. You can also create a label for a note and export it. The app isn't fancy; it's more for jotting down a phone number when you see a flyer about a missing kitten or making a quick note to yourself about what to pick up at the store, but for what it is, it's darn handy and easy to use.

Figure 11-7: Writing on your Kindle Fire HD screen is very freeing.

Exchange by TouchDown

From: NitroDesk, Inc.

Price: Free

If you want to access mail, contacts, and calendar information from your workplace and your company uses Microsoft Exchange Server for these accounts, this little app will help you tap into your company e-mail. It touts itself as providing great security and provides the very handy service of wiping data from your Kindle Fire HD remotely if it's lost or stolen.

Keep in mind that TouchDown doesn't work with IMAP or POP3 servers; it's intended for Exchange Servers. It supports Zimbra, Kerio, and ActiveSync, as well. Though the app has pretty easy-to-use settings (see Figure 11-8), you might want to sit down over a cup of coffee with your network administrator to get this one working. But when you do, we think you'll be pleased.

Figure 11-8: Make settings yourself or enlist the aid of your administrator.

Units

From: staticfree.info

Price: Free

If, like us, you need help converting just about anything to anything else (feet to meters, pounds to kilos, or whatever), you'll appreciate this handy little app. It handles 2,400 different conversions, including height, weight, volume, volume to weight, and time to distance. Tap the Unit key and you see a list of the various types of conversions available (see Figure 11-9).

Just fill in the You Have and You Want fields, and then enter the number of units. Tap the equal sign (=) and get your conversion. Holding Kindle Fire HD in landscape orientation displays a few more helpful tools on the calculator style interface.

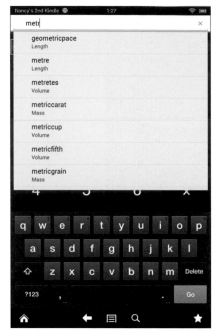

Figure 11-9: Tap the Unit key to get a list of common units.

Wi-Fi Analyzer

From: farproc

Price: Free

Because Kindle Fire HD can connect to the web only through Wi-Fi, this handy app is helpful for keeping track of local Wi-Fi connections. You can observe available Wi-Fi channels and the signal strength on each (see Figure 11-10). There are several styles of graph to choose from, including Channel, Time, Channel Rating, and Signal Meter.

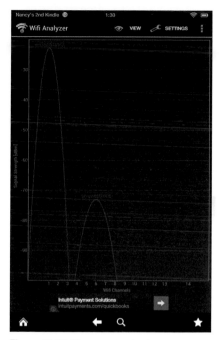

Figure 11-10: Figure out whether your nearest Wi-Fi will help you connect.

Chapter 12

Ten (or So) Top Gaming Apps

*P*eople using tablets will tell you that one of the great uses for them is to play games of all sorts. From card games such as solitaire to graphically entertaining new classics like Asphalt 7: Heat and Fruit Ninja, having access to games helps you while away a quiet evening at home or keep yourself from getting bored in boring settings, such as the security line at the airport or the dentist's waiting room.

Be sure to check out GameCircle, Amazon's new combination of social networking and gaming. Open the Games library and tap Connect to connect through Facebook and find friends who are using Amazon GameCircle. You can then share scores, achievements, and the games that you love to play with others.

In this chapter, we introduce you to 11 great games that will provide hours of fun and create the core of your Kindle Fire gaming library.

Cut the Rope

From: Zepto Lab

Price: $0.99

This is a very addictive game (ask author Nancy's husband; Nancy is a Cut the Rope widow). The whole idea is that there's this monster you have to feed candy to (don't ask why). The candy swings on ropes (see Figure 12-1) and you have to figure out how to cut the rope so that the candy whacks into various star-shaped objects, exploding them. The candy eventually ends up in the monster's mouth.

Figure 12-1: Figure out which rope to cut to whack the stars and feed the monster.

Along the way, you encounter various devices, such as little air blowers or balloons that help you manipulate items on the screen and achieve your goals. Fortunately, you're free to turn off the annoying music and sounds that seem to come from the candy. In the Menu setting on the Options bar, tap the little speaker to mute the sound. Then have fun feeding the monster!

Plants vs. Zombies

From: PopCap Games, Inc.

Price: $2.99

If you're somebody who worries about zombies attacking your home (and who doesn't?), this game will appeal to you. A phalanx of zombies waits on the street outside your house. You get to put plants in your front lawn to spit little seeds to cut down the zombies as they approach. You have to tap small suns that appear to help grow new plants that you can then place on your lawn to defeat yet more zombie attacks (see Figure 12-2).

Figure 12-2: Oh, no! Stop those zombies in their tracks!

As you proceed through levels of the game, you get additional items, such as sunflowers, walnuts, and Venus flytraps, that you can use in your attempts to thwart the zombies. At some point, you're told that the final wave of zombies is coming; if you survive the next minute or so, the zombies are defeated, and you get a new type of plant to use in your next defense against them.

Don't ask why. Just try it.

Fruit Ninja

From: HalfBrick Studios Pty Ltd.

Price: $0.99

This game combines the concept of a ninja warrior and fresh fruit. We think that this combination somehow makes the mayhem that ensues less violent in nature. Essentially, pieces of fruit are thrown up on the screen, and you use your finger to swipe across them, cutting them in half (see Figure 12-3). The trick is that occasionally a bomb gets thrown up with the fruit, and you have to be quick enough to not swipe at the bomb; otherwise, you blow it up and end the game with fruit salad everywhere.

Figure 12-3: Who knew that slicing fruit could be so fun?

If bombs aren't your thing, you can play the Zen mode, where you're merely slicing up fruit with no bombs involved. If you've had a hard day at the office, trust us, this one is great to work out your tensions. (Just imagine that the fruit is, well, anybody or anything that really annoyed you today.)

Quell Reflect

From: Fallen Tree Games

Price: $0.99

Quell is a peaceful afternoon in the park compared to some of the other games listed here. It doesn't involve bombs or zombies. Instead, you get a playing board with a small raindrop on it. You can move the raindrop up or down a row to collect the pearly objects in its path while peaceful Asian music plays in the background.

The trick is that you have to figure out how to get the raindrop to hit objects not already in its path. Sometimes you have to shift the raindrop from one side of the board to the other, move up, then over, then down, and so on until you're in line with the object you want to hit (see Figure 12-4).

As you proceed through levels, you get new challenges that require some brain power. But the whole experience is much more relaxing and peaceful than many games you find these days.

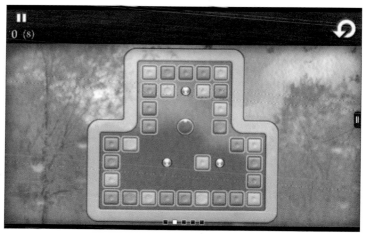

Figure 12-4: This little brain teaser will keep your mind sharp.

Airport Mania for Kindle Fire

From: Amazon Digital Services

Price: Free

Imagine that you're an air traffic controller. You sit in front of your Kindle Fire screen, allowing incoming planes to land, taxi to the terminal, let passengers off, move to a holding area, and take off again. Sounds easy, right?

It is until you have five or six planes coming in and out. Then it becomes seriously like rubbing your stomach while patting your head as a tornado approaches (see Figure 12-5). But give it a try. Nothing really crashes and nobody dies, so what can you lose?

One nice option in this game is the ability to turn the annoying music off but leave the cool sound effects on.

Figure 12-5: This game turns multitasking into an art form.

Jetpack Joyride

From: Halfbrick Studios Pty Ltd

Price: Free

Figure 12-6: Fly around with a jetpack and save the world!

The beauty of this game is that it really tests your reflexes as you get around obstacles in the skies and on land and avoid various physical threats.

Chess Free

From: Optime Software

Price: Free

If chess is your thing, you'll enjoy this electronic version. You can play the computer or play against another person using the same Kindle Fire. With the latter approach, the board swaps around after each play so that the next person can take his or her turn. There's a game timer if you're in Chess Tournament mode. You can also change the style of the pieces and board.

When you tap a piece, the game shows you all possible moves unless you turn off Show Legal and Last Moves in the game's Options. Tap the place on the board where you want to move the piece (see Figure 12-7). If you have a change of heart, this game includes a handy Undo button.

Figure 12-7: If you love chess, try this version.

Jewels

From: MH Games / Mika Haittunen

Price: Free

If you have a thing about jewelry, or even if you don't, you might enjoy Jewels. This matching game lets you play with jewel-colored baubles to your heart's content. The idea is that you can flip two gems on this grid-like game board if doing so will allow you to line up three items of the same kind (see Figure 12-8). When you do, the lines of gems shift to provide a different arrangement.

Figure 12-8: Simple yet colorful, Jewels promises hours of fun.

The game has a few other rules, involving getting more points for chain reactions and scoring bonus points. The game is over when no more possible three-of-a-kind matches remain.

Wordsmith

From: Second Breakfast Studios

Price: $2.49

Wordsmith is kind of like the popular word game Scrabble. You build words from available tiles and take advantage of double-letter and triple-word tiles (as shown in Figure 12-9) to score extra points.

The game definitely gets you thinking about how to utilize tiles already in place to one-up yourself or your opponent. The game accommodates two to four players. Build up your vocabulary while having fun with Wordsmith.

Figure 12-9: Scrabble fan alert! Wordsmith gets your spelling mojo on.

As with many games, this one comes in a free version as well. Free versions may include advertisements and offer more limited levels of play.

Solitaire Free Pack

From: Tesseract Mobile Software

Price: Free

You won't find too many surprises with this game, but for those who are devoted to solitaire, it offers an electronic version that you can play on the go on your Kindle Fire (see Figure 12-10). Rack up the points with 43 different games, including Klondike, Pyramid, and Monte Carlo.

You can change the card backgrounds and track your game scores to see whether you're improving as you go. If you want, you can take advantage of the unlimited redo feature to try and try again to win a game.

Figure 12-10: If you're alone, try a round of solitaire.

Asphalt 7: Heat

From: Gameloft

Price: $0.99

If you love to race fast cars, this game will give you that experience on your Kindle Fire HD with sharp graphics and quick moves. You can play around with more than 150 races in a wide variety of settings. You can play locally on your Kindle Fire HD or play with up to six people online in a multiplayer environment.

Do you fancy a DeLorean, a Ferrari, or a Lamborghini? They're all available here to test drive on tracks from Paris to Hawaii. But beware: This game has drop-dead gorgeous graphics (see Figure 12-11), but the trade-off is that you'll eat up about 20MB of your device's storage.

Figure 12-11: Race against the clock, or other drivers, in this fast-paced game!

And one for the traditional gamers

We like Random Mahjong (Paul Burkey, Free) because it has no time limits and no super bonus points to earn. You just take your time matching the nicely designed tiles layer by layer. You can control the look of the game and get hints when your brain is getting tired.

Index

Apple & Mac

iPad 2 For Dummies,
3rd Edition
978-1-118-17679-5

iPhone 4S
For Dummies,
5th Edition
978-1-118-03671-6

iPod touch
For Dummies,
3rd Edition
978-1-118-12960-9

Mac OS X Lion
For Dummies
978-1-118-02205-4

Blogging & Social Media

CityVille
For Dummies
978-1-118-08337-6

Facebook
For Dummies,
4th Edition
978-1-118-09562-1

Mom Blogging
For Dummies
978-1-118-03843-7

Twitter
For Dummies,
2nd Edition
978-0-470-76879-2

WordPress
For Dummies,
4th Edition
978-1-118-07342-1

Business

Cash Flow
For Dummies
978-1-118-01850-7

Investing
For Dummies,
6th Edition
978-0-470-90545-6

Job Searching with
Social Media
For Dummies
978-0-470-93072-4

QuickBooks 2012
For Dummies
978-1-118-09120-3

Resumes
For Dummies,
6th Edition
978-0-470-87361-8

Starting an Etsy
Business For Dummies
978-0-470-93067-0

Cooking & Entertaining

Cooking Basics
For Dummies,
4th Edition
978-0-470-91388-8

Wine For Dummies,
4th Edition
978-0-470-04579-4

Diet & Nutrition

Kettlebells
For Dummies
978-0-470-59929-7

Nutrition
For Dummies,
5th Edition
978-0-470-93231-5

Restaurant
Calorie Counter
For Dummies,
2nd Edition
978-0-470-64405-8

Digital Photography

Digital SLR Cameras &
Photography
For Dummies,
4th Edition
978-1-118-14489-3

Digital SLR Settings
& Shortcuts
For Dummies
978-0-470-91763-3

Photoshop Elements 10
For Dummies
978-1-118-10742-3

Gardening

Gardening Basics
For Dummies
978-0-470-03749-2

Vegetable Gardening
For Dummies,
2nd Edition
978-0-470-49870-5

Green/Sustainable

Raising Chickens
For Dummies
978-0-470-46544-8

Green Cleaning
For Dummies
970-0-470 39106 8

Health

Diabetes For Dummies,
3rd Edition
978-0-470-27086-8

Food Allergies
For Dummies
978-0-470-09584-3

Living Gluten-Free
For Dummies,
2nd Edition
978-0-470-58589-4

Hobbies

Beekeeping
For Dummies,
2nd Edition
978-0-470-43065-1

Chess For Dummies,
3rd Edition
978-1-118-01695-4

Drawing
For Dummies,
2nd Edition
978-0-470-61842-4

eBay For Dummies,
7th Edition
978-1-118-09806-6

Knitting
For Dummies,
2nd Edition
978-0-470-28747-7

Language & Foreign Language

English Grammar
For Dummies,
2nd Edition
978-0-470-54664-2

French
For Dummies,
2nd Edition
978-1-118-00464-7

German
For Dummies,
2nd Edition
978-0-470-90101-4

Spanish Essentials
For Dummies
978-0-470-63751-7

Spanish
For Dummies,
2nd Edition
978-0-470-87855-2

Available wherever books are sold. For more information or to order direct: U.S. customers visit
www.dummies.com or call 1-877-762-2974. U.K. customers visit www.wileyeurope.com or
call (0) 1243 843291. Canadian customers visit www.wiley.ca or call 1-800-567-4797.
Connect with us online at www.facebook.com/fordummies or @fordummies

Math & Science

Algebra I
For Dummies,
2nd Edition
978-0-470-55964-2

Biology
For Dummies,
2nd Edition
978-0-470-59875-7

Chemistry
For Dummies,
2nd Edition
978-1-1180-0730-3

Geometry
For Dummies,
2nd Edition
978-0-470-08946-0

Pre-Algebra Essentials
For Dummies
978-0-470-61838-7

Microsoft Office

Excel 2010
For Dummies
978-0-470-48953-6

Office 2010 All-in-One
For Dummies
978-0-470-49748-7

Office 2011 for Mac
For Dummies
978-0-470-87869-9

Word 2010
For Dummies
978-0-470-48772-3

Music

Guitar
For Dummies,
2nd Edition
978-0-7645-9904-0

Clarinet For Dummies
978-0-470-58477-4

iPod & iTunes
For Dummies,
9th Edition
978-1-118-13060-5

Pets

Cats For Dummies,
2nd Edition
978-0-7645-5275-5

Dogs All-in One
For Dummies
978-0470-52978-2

Saltwater Aquariums
For Dummies
978-0-470-06805-2

Religion & Inspiration

The Bible
For Dummies
978-0-7645-5296-0

Catholicism
For Dummies,
2nd Edition
978-1-118-07778-8

Spirituality
For Dummies,
2nd Edition
978-0-470-19142-2

Self-Help & Relationships

Happiness
For Dummies
978-0-470-28171-0

Overcoming Anxiety
For Dummies,
2nd Edition
978-0-470-57441-6

Seniors

Crosswords
For Seniors
For Dummies
978-0-470-49157-7

iPad 2 For Seniors
For Dummies,
3rd Edition
978-1-118-17678-8

Laptops & Tablets
For Seniors
For Dummies,
2nd Edition
978-1-118-09596-6

Smartphones & Tablets

BlackBerry
For Dummies,
5th Edition
978-1-118-10035-6

Droid X2 For Dummies
978-1-118-14864-8

HTC ThunderBolt
For Dummies
978-1-118-07601-9

MOTOROLA XOOM
For Dummies
978-1-118-08835-7

Sports

Basketball
For Dummies,
3rd Edition
978-1-118-07374-2

Football
For Dummies,
2nd Edition
978-1-118-01261-1

Golf For Dummies,
4th Edition
978-0-470-88279-5

Test Prep

ACT For Dummies,
5th Edition
978-1-118-01259-8

ASVAB For Dummies,
3rd Edition
978-0-470-63760-9

The GRE Test
For Dummies,
7th Edition
978-0-470-00919-2

Police Officer Exam
For Dummies
978-0-470-88724-0

Series 7 Exam
For Dummies
978-0-470-09932-2

Web Development

HTML, CSS, & XHTML
For Dummies,
7th Edition
978-0-470-91659-9

Drupal For Dummies,
2nd Edition
978-1-118-08348-2

Windows 7

Windows 7
For Dummies
978-0-470-49743-2

Windows 7
For Dummies,
Book + DVD Bundle
978-0-470-52398-8

Windows 7 All-in-One
For Dummies
978-0-470-48763-1

Available wherever books are sold. For more information or to order direct: U.S. customers visit
www.dummies.com or call 1-877-762-2974. U.K. customers visit www.wileyeurope.com or
call (0) 1243 843291. Canadian customers visit www.wiley.ca or call 1-800-567-4797.
Connect with us online at www.facebook.com/fordummies or @fordummies